BLOODY SUNDAY

Contemporary Irish Studies

Series Editor: Peter Shirlow (School of Environmental Studies, University of Ulster, Coleraine)

Also available:

Edited by James Anderson and James Goodman
  Dis/Agreeing Ireland: Contexts, Obstacles, Hopes
Colin Coulter
  Contemporary Northern Irish Society: An Introduction
Graham Ellison and Jim Smyth
  The Crowned Harp: Policing Northern Ireland
Edited by Paul Hainsworth
  Divided Society: Ethnic Minorities and Racism in Northern Ireland
Edited by Peadar Kirby, Luke Gibbons and Michael Cronin
  Reinventing Ireland: Culture, Society and the Global Economy
Jim Mac Laughlin
  Imagining Ireland: The Contested Terrains of Irish Nation Building
Gerry Smyth
  Decolonisation and Criticism: The Construction of Irish Literature

Related titles:

Edited by Marie Smyth and Marie-Therese Fay
  Personal Accounts from Northern Ireland: Public Conflict, Private Loss
Mike Morrissey and Marie Smyth
  Northern Ireland after the Good Friday Agreement: Victims, Grievance and Blame
Edited by Marie Smyth and Gillian Robinson
  Researching Violently Divided Societies: Ethical and Methodological Issues
Colin Crawford, with an introduction by Marie Smyth
  Inside the UDA: Volunteers and Violence

Bloody Sunday
Trauma, Pain and Politics

Patrick Hayes and Jim Campbell

Pluto Press
London • Dublin • Ann Arbor, MI

First published 2005 by Pluto Press
345 Archway Road, London N6 5AA
and 839 Greene Street, Ann Arbor, MI 48106

Distributed in the Republic of Ireland and Northern Ireland by
Columba Mercier Distribution, 55A Spruce Avenue, Stillorgan Industrial Park,
Blackrock, Co. Dublin, Ireland. Tel: + 353 1 294 2556. Fax: + 353 1 294 2564

www.plutobooks.com

British Library Cataloguing in Publication Data
A catalogue record for this book is available from the British Library

Library of Congress Cataloging-in-Publication Data

Hayes, Patrick.
    Bloody Sunday : trauma, pain & politics / Patrick Hayes and Jim Campbell.
      p. cm. -- (Contemporary Irish studies)
    ISBN 0-7453-1854-1 -- ISBN 0-7453-1853-3 (pbk.)
    1. Derry (Northern Ireland)--History.
    2. Political violence--Northern Ireland--Derry--History--20th century.
    3. Demonstrations--Northern Ireland--Derry--History--20th century.
    4. Massacres--Northern Ireland--Derry--History--20th century.
    5. Post-traumatic stress disorder--Northern Ireland--Derry.
    6. Derry (Northern Ireland)--Social conditions.
    I. Campbell, Jim, 1956- II. Title. III. Series.
    DA995.L75H39 2003
    941.6'210824--dc21

                                                                    2002152364

                        10 9 8 7 6 5 4 3 2 1

                    ISBN 0 7453 1854 1 hardback
                    ISBN 0 7453 1853 3 paperback

        Designed and produced for Pluto Press by Curran Publishing Services
                    Printed and bound in the European Union by
                Antony Rowe Ltd, Chippenham and Eastbourne, England

Contents

CONTENTS

CONTENTS

Figures and Tables

Figure

Tables

The authors dedicate this work to the memory of the 14 men who lost their lives as a result of shootings on the streets of Derry, 30 January 1972 during a civil rights march and to their families, their children and future generations who will continue to work with courage and dignity to achieve justice in order that they may grieve their dead.

Acknowledgements

We are particularly grateful to all the Bloody Sunday family members who offered their hospitality and friendship, and shared their stories that made the completion of this book possible. Particular thanks are accorded to Dr John Pinkerton and Dr Karola Dillenburger of Queen's University Belfast for their advice and encouragement at different stages of the research and writing up process. Dr Marie Smyth of the University of Ulster and INCORE provided the initial impetus for the project in Derry and deserves special thanks. Linda Nash-Roddy, whose brother William was killed on Bloody Sunday, gave a great deal of her time and effort in helping with the research, and introduced us to so many other family members. Without this invaluable relationship, this book would not have been possible. Sharon Meenan kindly permitted us to print the poem in the frontmatter. We also wish to thank Julie Stoll and Roger van Zwanenburg from Pluto Press for their help and patience in working with us towards the book's conclusion, and Rosaleen Gormley for her secretarial expertise. Finally the authors wish to acknowledge their wives, Eileen Hayes and Anona Campbell, for their love and support.

I Wasn't Even Born

I remember people happy and the confidence of that morning.
The Creggan Shops.
I remember the banner that was carried. The gathered message.
I remember live fire.
A pool of blood on the pavement.
I remember Hugh Gilmore and Patrick Doherty.
I remember running. The Flats.
I remember Jim Wray and Michael McDaid.
I remember screaming.
English accents.
I remember William Nash and Gerard McKinney.
I remember a crazed army.
A white hanky.
I remember Michael Kelly and John Young.
I remember it black and white. But blood is always red.
I remember Jackie Duddy and Bernard McGuigan.
I remember looking for my friend from the confusion and then
through the quiet.
I remember Gerard Donaghy and Kevin McElhinney.
I remember hearing the news.
I remember John Johnston and William McKinney.
I remember thirteen coffins. Black flags.
I remember a young woman with an old face.
The funerals.
I remember my father crying hot, angry tears.
I remember the lies.
And I wasn't even born.

Killian Mullan and Sharon Meenan, Derry, 1997
used with permission.

Introduction

On 30 January 1972, in Derry,[1] Northern Ireland, 13 unarmed male civilians were killed by the British Parachute Regiment during a banned civil rights demonstration. Another man died later from gunshot wounds received that day. This event, commonly known as 'Bloody Sunday', is marked yearly with anniversary commemorations. Although it happened in 1972, recurring press coverage of the original events, the ongoing 'Troubles' (a term commonly used to describe the conflict in Northern Ireland over the past 35 years), recent family attempts to seek redress, anniversary marches, and the commission of the Saville Inquiry to establish the truth of what happened that day mean that Bloody Sunday is frequently recalled and referred to by people in Northern Ireland.

The significance of the incident is such that it is also regularly discussed in general literature on the Troubles and a number of specific books have been written about this subject over the years. Most of these have sought to 'tell the truth' about the events to correct the perceived inaccuracies and injustices which flowed from the Widgery Tribunal which was convened in the months immediately following Bloody Sunday to investigate the events of the day (HMSO, 1972). The writings range from personal and journalistic, to legal accounts of the period before, during and after the event: McClean's (1997) *The Road to Bloody Sunday*; McCann, Shiels and Hannigan's (1992) *Bloody Sunday in Derry*; McCafferty's (1989) *Peggy Deery*; Pringle and Jacobson's (2000) *Those Are Real Bullets, Aren't They?*; Mullan's (1997) *Eyewitness Bloody Sunday*; and Walsh's (2000) *Bloody Sunday and the Rule of Law in Northern Ireland*. These texts manage to piece together the story of the day through eyewitnesses or in the stories of family members and the wider community. What emerge are compelling accounts of human pain and tragedy, as well as political and legal contributions that seek to reveal substantive injustices.

The impetus for *Bloody Sunday: Trauma, Pain and Politics* arose from the convergence of two sets of personal experiences. Patrick Hayes spent the first nine years of his life in the Bogside, Derry,

[1]

the densely populated Catholic area of the city that was to become the site of Bloody Sunday some three decades later. His interest in psychological trauma acquired as a psychotherapist for many years in the United States prompted him to inquire about how the event may have affected the Derry community, in particular families who had been bereaved. A preliminary study (Smyth and Hayes, 1994) indicated that substantial levels of trauma may exist among the Bloody Sunday families whose relatives were killed. Family members, some of whom witnessed violence and were subjected to life threatening danger, were still living in the community and subjected to daily reminders of their trauma. This initial work encouraged Hayes to carry out an in-depth investigation as part of his doctoral research at the Queen's University of Belfast (Hayes, 2000). Jim Campbell, who became involved in the project as supervisor of the thesis, has spent all of his life in Northern Ireland and was aged 16 and living in Belfast at the time of Bloody Sunday. He was brought up within a Protestant, Unionist family who, like many others at the time, assumed that the state must have had good reason to have killed and injured protestors. His subsequent interest in researching the effects of the Troubles on health and social care services coincided with a concern, shared with Patrick Hayes, that there was a need to re-examine the social, psychological and political impact of Bloody Sunday on family members.

Bloody Sunday: Trauma, Pain and Politics seeks to build upon other accounts by offering a different, but complementary, approach to this significant event in the history of Northern Ireland. It uses a primarily qualitative methodology complemented by two quantitative measures, to examine the narrative content of interviews carried out with family members of those who were killed on Bloody Sunday. It is important from the outset to explain that this account is necessarily partial for a number of reasons. It is not possible to generalise findings from this study and apply them to all families who lost a relative on Bloody Sunday, let alone other groups of people who have suffered because of the violence in Northern Ireland. Qualitative research by its nature seeks to explore and construct meaning from interview data provided by subsections of wider populations. For this reason we can only seek to summarise and analyse the views of

[2]

the sample of Bloody Sunday families who participated in the study. We were not involved in exploring many other important issues around Bloody Sunday, for example the relatively neglected area of those who had been injured, or the task of establishing the facts of the day that have been comprehensively discussed in the books identified above.

We also must acknowledge, as others who have carried out research into violent conflicts have done (Smyth and Robinson, 2001), that we did not come to this study as neutral observers of a traumatic event. The important point here is not so much that bias is inherent in much social research, we know this to be the case, but that implicit values and assumptions should be brought to the open, acknowledged and factored into subsequent claims made by researchers (Dawes, Tredoux and Feinstein, 1989). Although we have quite contrasting biographies and life experiences, we generally agree that the way the state behaved on Bloody Sunday was unjust and that subsequent neglect of the issue, and more importantly the suffering of victims as a result of it, was wrong. We believe that, in such situations, it is important to find a way in which those who have suffered can have a voice. The opportunity to tell these stories in this text is just one of a number of ways that family members can have their views heard.

Hayes' study provides the framework for this book about the event that many believe served as the catalyst for the most recent round of political violence in Northern Ireland that has spanned more than 30 years. Research from other parts of the world suggest that one way of coping with trauma is to integrate it into one's life story (Aron, 1992; Hadden, Rutherford and Merrette, 1978; Herbst, 1992; Hunt, 1997; McGoldrick, 1995; Nagata, 1990; Shepherd, 1992; Solkoff, 1981; Solkoff, 1992; van der Kolk, 1994; van der Kolk and Fisler, 1995; Weine et al., 1995). For example, telling the story to one's children will inform them of what happened, may illuminate confusion about family members' behaviour related to the trauma, and may promote their general health (McGoldrick, 1995; Nagata, 1990; van der Kolk, 1994; van der Kolk and Fisler, 1995). This book presents the stories of a sample of surviving family members illustrating unresolved grief complicated by ongoing trauma, which may have intergenerational consequences. It also reveals traumatic memories of the day and of lost family members, inter-group conflict, views on politics and society, health and social care, and perceptions about the Saville Inquiry.

In writing this book we wished to avoid viewing Bloody Sunday as an isolated incident, somehow detached from the maelstrom of social, economic and political events that have occurred in the last 30 or more years. For this reason, we provide an overview of theoretical and historical perspectives related to trauma and politics which are helpful when we begin to interpret the complexity of individual and family narratives.

Chapter 1 sets Bloody Sunday in context by providing an overview of the historical backdrop of the Troubles in Northern Ireland. This includes an account of competing political, ethnic/ cultural and economic perspectives on the causes of the Troubles, and the problems that flowed from the partition of Ireland in 1921. The specific circumstances of Derry in the late 1960s and early 1970s are outlined, with a particular emphasis on the geo-politics of the city, sectarian discrimination and increasing civil unrest leading to the events of Bloody Sunday. Bloody Sunday is also discussed in the context of many other traumatic incidents caused by political violence, which occurred in the last 30-plus years. All these events, and many more, led to multiple deaths, injuries and subsequent trauma and also raise important ethical and political questions about victimhood. Without denying the very real and acutely painful suffering experienced by other individuals, families and communities caught up in these terrible events, it is argued that Bloody Sunday was of special significance, because of the nature of state involvement in the killings, a flawed, inadequate and suspect investigation into the killings, and the profound impact the incident had on fuelling subsequent paramilitary and state violence.

A variety of perspectives have been used to explain the nature of state violence, both in Northern Ireland and elsewhere in the world. We believe that a critical exploration of the role of state in society is important in explaining how events like Bloody Sunday happen and the resulting traumatic consequences for victims.

Chapter 2 begins by highlighting competing discourses on violence for and against the state using international examples. Of particular interest to the authors is the way in which states, before and after the events of 9/11, presented their worldview on the causes of insurgency. The chapter then focuses on the specific context of state violence in Northern Ireland, from the early periods of the Troubles in the 1920s and 1930s to the more recent events of the last three decades. It is argued that throughout this period the state often used excessive violence and repressive law to deal with insurgencies and street violence. It is only in recent years, following the Belfast Agreement in 1998, that opportunities are beginning to emerge to explore and address the impact of such violence. The chapter concludes by reflecting upon ways in which the state can deal with past injustices which may lead to the resolution of trauma suffered by groups such as the Bloody Sunday families.

A central issue raised throughout this book is the complex relationship between political violence and trauma. Chapter 3 reviews literature on the concept of trauma, with a particular focus on the term Posttraumatic Stress Disorder (PTSD). The works of contemporary thinkers such as Horowitz, van der Kolk, Herman, and others, provide a basis for understanding PTSD. It is also recognised that earlier views on PTSD need to be modified by recognising the impact of biological, social, environmental and political determinants. The chapter also examines the interaction between grief and mourning and trauma, ways of helping those affected by trauma, and research about the concept in the context of Northern Ireland. The importance of narrative as part of a healing process is also highlighted in the literature.

Chapter 4 discusses the framework for the study methodology and the rationale for using a primarily qualitative, narrative approach complemented by two measures, one which examined evidence of possible PTSD symptomatology and the second, the General Health Questionnaire-12 (GHQ-12) which measured aspects of general health. The study sample is described along with procedures and data analysis for both qualitative and quantitative approaches. Findings from the measures are reported and provide an explanatory backdrop for interpreting the narratives. Chapters 5, 6, 8 and 10, and parts of Chapter 7, concentrate on the description and analysis of the accounts that were provided by family members. Data was coded into coherent themes and theoretical perspectives related to trauma, grief and mourning, and storytelling is used to explain and interpret narratives.

Chapter 5 presents stories about the day of Bloody Sunday told in the actual words of relatives of the victims at the time of the 25th anniversary. The intense and compelling imagery in the language reveals a sense of the intractability of the trauma resulting from the perception of helplessness, injustice and betrayal along with the horrific realisation that one's life is at imminent risk. The immediate aftermath of the event, including family shock at learning of the deaths, followed by the funerals that appeared to paralyse, not only the families, but also the wider Derry community, is poignantly described. These events set the stage for incomplete grieving and for potential continuous traumatic stress.

In Chapter 6 narratives, a range of phenomena emerge in the aftermath of trauma: feelings of irrevocable loss, not just of the family member, but of future generations; loss of one's identity as an individual which was subsumed into the collective identity of being a Bloody Sunday family member; loss of innocence, faith, security, childhood, trust, and family celebrations and rituals. A sense of betrayal and injustice following the findings of Widgery Tribunal and harassment by security forces compounded the trauma and the grieving process for the lost relative. Other themes that became evident included attitudes towards politics and the way in which parenting styles and coping were affected. This was the case not only for parents who lost a son and who were rearing their other children in the years immediately following Bloody Sunday, but also for the siblings and children of those killed as they became parents of a new generation many years later. In the face of loss, the general family response was to protect the next generation through silence about Bloody Sunday and by instilling an anti-violent, apolitical ethic in their children. These strategies may have been used to protect family members from future loss. The Bloody Sunday Justice Campaign often became a support for family members and provided them with a means to seek justice for the death of their family member.

Subsequent chapters of the book include a focus on the way the state generally failed to respond to the social and psychological needs of those who have been traumatised in these ways.

In Chapter 7, the history of health and social care services during the Troubles in Northern Ireland is critically analysed. It is argued that there continue to be problems for groups who have been victimised or see themselves as being victimised by the state, when the state is perceived as the perpetrator of the violence. Nonetheless, current political and social change in Northern Ireland, along with new developments in the provision of health and social welfare, may provide some help to those, like the Bloody Sunday families, who have suffered. The views are tested by reference to some of the narratives collected during the second stage of interviews in 2001.

Chapter 8 includes an update of findings from interviews carried out with some of the original cohort of families five years after the original study at the time of the 25th anniversary. Family members were asked to talk about their views on the events that has transpired in Northern Ireland since that time, especially the peace process and the emergence of the new inquiry into the events of Bloody Sunday. Family members shared perceptions of the peace process, changes in the Derry community attitudes towards Bloody Sunday and the media, and the impact of the Saville Inquiry on family members and the Derry community. Their narratives suggest that the Inquiry might deal with some longstanding concerns and may help in some aspects of trauma resolution; however, this alone will not be a panacea for all of the ills that flowed from Bloody Sunday.

Because questions remain for many of the families about the resolution of issues surrounding and subsequent to the events of Bloody Sunday, Chapter 9 focuses on the background to and the processes involved in the establishment of the Saville Inquiry and whether this process is likely to mitigate or exacerbate the trauma or lead to resolution of issues related to truth and justice for family members. The peace process in Northern Ireland appears to have fostered an environment which was more favourable for considering a re-examination of the events of Bloody Sunday and for addressing the flaws of the Widgery Tribunal.

The conclusions of the Widgery Tribunal, which was hastily convened and concluded shortly after Bloody Sunday, left family members and the Derry community with a profound sense of injustice, victim blaming, and a conviction that the truth would never be learned about what happened that day. Prime Minister Tony Blair announced the setting up of the new Saville Inquiry which began its work on 3 April 1998. This has been the most expensive and exhaustive investigation into such an event in the history of the British state. The chapter concludes by suggesting that the Inquiry alone is unlikely to resolve all the guilt, blame, and needs for reparation that stemmed from Bloody Sunday or from other painful events during the recent Troubles in Northern Ireland.

Chapter 10 recounts family members' experiences, hopes and fears for the outcome as testimony unfolded in the day-to-day events of the Inquiry. Respondents generally found the help and support of other family members, and the wider Derry community, to be comforting as some questions which had remained unanswered for so long were addressed. Family members acknowledged that, despite intense distress at hearing testimony about loved ones' deaths and at times, frustration with the conduct of the Inquiry, it was 'worth it' if truth and justice will be served.

The conclusion draws together a variety of themes that arose in the book. We argue that a number of important issues were raised in the course of the research, including a sense that many of the respondents were still experiencing symptoms of posttraumatic stress, grief, guilt, loss, anger and injustice about an event which happened more than 30 years ago. Nonetheless, there were optimistic accounts about hopes for the future and a willingness to try to move on. What concerned some respondents were the dangers of another perceived compromise which might emerge from the Saville Inquiry that may simply echo the injustices of the Widgery Tribunal. This raises the possibility of once again compounding the original trauma of Bloody Sunday. The authors argue that there is a need for broader policy approaches in helping individuals, families and communities who, like the Bloody Sunday families, have suffered so much during the Troubles. This may include more comprehensive, sensitive services, but also mechanisms for allowing people who have been traumatised to understand and talk about the past.

Note

1 The authors use the name Derry to describe the city because it was the common description used by respondents and many other citizens. We wish to recognise, however, that a sizeable minority of the city's population have the right to express their own sense of identity and citizenship by referring to it as Londonderry.

1 Bloody Sunday in context

While Bloody Sunday in Derry is but one event in the history of Northern Ireland, it played an important role in the escalation of the recent Troubles, which have their roots in centuries of political and social conflict. In recognising this past, it is also important to acknowledge that any attempt to describe it will necessarily be partial and value-laden. There is no one history of Ireland; instead multiple, contested versions exist from which to choose (Farrell, 1992; Stewart, 1977; Foster, 1988). The same can be said of contemporary analyses of the current conflict and its causes. What we have are significant events which are viewed, interpreted and reconstructed by institutions and social forces. What is provided below is a brief interpretation of what we believe are relevant factors in a long history of political violence. This, we believe, will help contextualise significant events which occurred before and after Bloody Sunday, and provide background detail to the chapters which follow.

The origins of the conflict

Much has been written about the origins of the conflict, which has lasted for at least 600 years. A significant factor in this history has been the impact of English colonialism on early modern Ireland which led, in turn, to conflict between the indigenous population and settlers from the island of Britain. Although the relationship between the metropolitan centre and the colonised island of Ireland entailed various degrees of exploitation and oppression, it would be too simple to describe these processes as linear and one-dimensional.

The plantation of Ireland took place in different historical phases involving a complex set of social, economic and political factors. What emerged from these experiences are what Foster (1988) describes as 'varieties of Irishness' in which Planter and Gael, at various periods in history, both clashed and coexisted. It was, however, the particular character of the plantation in the province of Ulster in the northeast which created the conditions for sectarian violence from the seventeenth century onwards. The Williamite revolution established the primacy of the Protestant faith, although the established Anglican Church continued to battle with nonconformists as well as Catholics until after the rebellion of the United Irishmen failed in the late eighteenth century. The impact of the Industrial Revolution also had a profound effect on socio-economic relationships in Ulster, suggesting to some that the lack of such development elsewhere on the island created conditions for the maintenance and replication of sectarian violence and inequality (Bew, Gibbon and Patterson, 1996; McVeigh, 1997).

By the nineteenth century the growing demand for an independent Irish nationhood created a dilemma for Unionists on the island, who were mostly concentrated in the nine counties of the traditional province of Ulster and the area around Dublin. Unsuccessful attempts in the late nineteenth century to introduce a series of Home Rule bills at Westminster, mass resistance to Home Rule in Ulster prior to the First World War, the Easter Rising during that war, and the subsequent Anglo-Irish War of 1919–21, were key moments in a process that ultimately led to the partition of Ireland in 1921. The Government of Ireland Act created the state of Northern Ireland with the old province of Ulster, now reduced to six counties but with an in-built Protestant and Unionist majority. Northern Ireland remained constitutionally part of the United Kingdom, whilst the new Free State was provided a large degree of independence under the Treaty conditions, but still with only dominion status.

These new political and constitutional arrangements marked Northern Ireland out as a contested geopolitical space, 'a place apart' within the United Kingdom. Many Catholics, who constituted a large minority of Northern Ireland's population, perceived themselves as Nationalists 'trapped'; their political aspirations to be part of the new Republic of Ireland in the 26 southern counties were hardly recognised during most of the 50-year period of the local devolved administration at Stormont. Conversely, most Protestants saw the Union within the United Kingdom as a guarantee of civil and political rights and felt threatened by what appeared to be an alien and hostile culture in the Free State, and later the Republic of Ireland.

Interestingly, the city of Londonderry (the city council changed its name to Derry in 1984) has played a central role in the history of Ireland, before and after partition. The site of the current city on the banks of the Foyle hosted centuries of Gaelic culture before the extensive plantation of the county of Londonderry in the sixteenth and seventeenth centuries. The original Gaelic name had become anglicised by the addition of the prefix 'London' when artisans and tradesmen from London guilds colonised the region and constructed the city walls to protect against native Irish attack. Crucially, it was the siege of Derry and the role that the Apprentice Boys played in holding out against the forces of the Catholic king, James, which established an important myth in Protestant Unionist culture, which remains to this day. In the centuries that followed, Catholics tended to be marginalised, excluded from the city walls and located in poorer lands to the west of the city, including the Bogside.

Simplistic notions of national identity, religious affiliation and ethnic difference cannot, however, fully explain the history of the political conflict in Northern Ireland. There have been, for example, various moments in Northern Irish history when nationality has not been an organising principle around which politics revolve. For example, the motivation of class interest can help explain the revolt of the United Irishmen in 1798, the Poor Law Relief riots in Belfast in 1933 and the rise of the Northern Ireland Labour Party in the 1960s. Although some academic and political discourses reinforce the notion that the conflict in Northern Ireland is essentially one of 'two warring tribes', the role of the British, and, to a lesser extent the Irish political establishment in managing, and at times exacerbating, the conflict, should not be ignored (Whyte, 1991; McGarry and O'Leary, 1995).

The weakness of the local economy has also been a contributory factor in this political instability. Although industrial activity was characterised by dynamic periods during the nineteenth century, the manufacturing base went into almost continuous decline in the twentieth century (Borooah, 1993). As a result the Northern Ireland state depended upon subventions from Westminster in order to deliver a wide range of spending commitments on social security, health and education, agriculture, industry, and defence. High levels of unemployment, poverty and a range of unmet health and social needs have been features of the political economy of Northern Ireland. When statistics on inequality are disaggregated, some groups are shown to have been worse off than others. For example, concepts of indirect and direct discrimination have been used to explain why Catholics continue to be more than twice as likely as Protestants to be unemployed (Teague, 1993; McGarry and O'Leary, 1995). Westminster's disregard of the internal affairs of Northern Ireland since its inception in 1921 allowed a form of politics to develop that is typified by sectarian conflict (McVeigh, 1997). Even the geopolitics of the region reflect such divisions, with Catholics tending to live in the west and Protestants in the east. Thus, the people in Derry, where Bloody Sunday took place, have been multiply disadvantaged. This is partly because the region's natural trading hinterland was blocked by the erection of the border in 1921, and also because industrial and commercial policies tended to focus on the interests of the population in the east of Northern Ireland (Probert, 1978: 54).

Northern Ireland: a contested state

From the outset, the devolved administration in Northern Ireland faced many difficulties: a continuous threat of insurgency and the existence of a very large minority (about one third) of its citizens who generally looked across the new border for national identity and allegiance. These precarious beginnings for the new state may explain, but do not excuse, the use by successive governments of repressive laws and policing, and the gerrymandering of electoral districts (Walsh, 2000). In addition, a system of economic discrimination often disadvantaged the large, mostly Catholic Nationalist minority, whilst leaving many working-class Unionists also impoverished (Bew, Gibbon and Patterson, 1996). Violence was an ever-present feature of the state in its early years. For example, between June 1920 and June 1922, 428 people lost their lives in a spate of sectarian violence; two-thirds of these were Catholics (McKittrick and McVea, 2001: 4).

It has been argued that social changes introduced by the Westminster government after the Second World War, especially free secondary education, led to the rise of a Catholic middle class, which began to assert its right to civil and political liberties. This assertion of rights, in turn, appeared to threaten the relatively advantaged positions held by many Protestants (Darby, 1995). Bew, Gibbon and Patterson (1996: 146–58), however, challenge the notion that a developing, monolithic Catholic middle class was so influential. A more plausible explanation for increasing radicalism involves a fuller consideration of the complexity of Northern Irish society at the time:

> While growing in numbers, the [Catholic] middle class actually remained remarkable more for its conservative than for its radical qualities. The situation was rather one in which the social basis, the political space and the impetus and the opportunity of apparent success for a middle class reform movement all coincided.
>
> (Bew, Gibbon and Patterson, 1996: 154)

What is not in doubt was the further polarisation that occurred in the late 1960s when calls by the civil rights movement for an end to discrimination in housing, employment and electoral abuses were resisted by the state and most of the Unionist community (Arthur, 1974; Purdy, 1990). The ensuing civil disorder led to the deployment of British soldiers on the streets of Northern Ireland by the Westminster administration in 1969 and 30 long years of civil and political violence followed.

Civil rights, increasing violence and internment

This early period of the present conflict in Northern Ireland was characterised by an increase in community tension and a greater willingness by the state and its opponents to resort to violence. For example, 18 people died in 1969, 26 in 1970 and 186 in 1971 (Fay, Morrissey and Smyth, 1999: 137). During these years this wider conflict within the state inevitably impinged on the lives of people living in Derry, Northern Ireland's second largest city. For example, one of the earliest civil rights demonstrations to gain the attention of the international news media occurred when around 400 activists, including local members of parliament, organised an illegal march from the Waterside to the Diamond in the Cityside on 5 October 1968. In the violence that followed, the Royal Ulster Constabulary (RUC) baton-charged and used water cannons on protesters, leaving 100 to seek hospital attention (Pringle and Jacobson, 2000: 33). In a Northern Ireland Civil Rights Association (NICRA) march from Belfast to Derry in early January 1969, Unionist counter-protesters and the RUC attacked marchers at Burntollet Bridge, leaving many injured. As in other parts of Northern Ireland, such events served to reinforce a sense of help-lessness and anger, leading to further civil unrest in Derry. The city became the site for regular battles between rioters and the RUC, and increasing involvement of the Irish Republican Army (IRA) in attacks on police.

In particular, a great deal of local conflict and violence was centred on the Catholic *enclave* of the Bogside which saw increasing violence between the Nationalist community on one side, and the RUC and British Army on the other. The entrenched nature of this conflict, and how it permeated the local community is graphically represented by the mural on 'Free Derry Corner' of a child wearing a gas mask, involved in a riot. The 'Battle of the Bogside', as it became known, left a substantial area of the city in open revolt against the forces of law and order which eventually led to the intro-duction of the British Army (Walsh, 2000: 37–8). The battle involved three days of intense protests and rioting that followed a traditional, Protestant Apprentice Boys' march on 12 August 1969. The volun-tary, part-time wing of the RUC, known as the 'B Specials' was heavily implicated in violence which ensued, and order could not be restored. When riots broke out in Belfast and elsewhere in North-ern Ireland, the Stormont administration was forced to appeal to Westminster for army support. Whatever perception there might have been by most Catholics at the time that this was a necessary act which may have initially helped to prevent attacks and violence, the assumption that the army could act as neutral arbiters, separate either from central or local government policy making, quickly evaporated.

The following two years were characterised by cycles of violence involving the security forces, the IRA and local commu-nities. For example, 1,800 families, of whom 1,500 were Catholics, were forced to flee their homes mostly in north and west Belfast in late summer 1969. A curfew was placed on the Falls Road in July

1970 and there was a growing presence of paramilitary activity in violent incidents (McKittrick and McVea, 2001, chapter 3). Derry was not immune from the escalating conflict. In the summer of 1970 three members of the IRA blew themselves up whilst constructing a bomb in the Creggan (a Catholic housing area in Derry) also killing two local girls. Bombings and shootings became a regular occurrence in the city as in other areas of Northern Ireland (Pringle and Jacobson, 2000: 41–2).

On 9 August 1971 the policy of internment, designed as a last effort by the devolved administration towards quelling civil disturbance related to civil rights protests, was implemented throughout Northern Ireland with the support of the British Army. Over a three- month period, 1,882 men, mostly Catholics and all Nationalists, were interned without charge for unlimited periods (McCann, Shiels and Hannigan, 1992). By the start of 1972 this figure had risen to 2,400; again nearly all Catholic men. Although the Prime Minister of Northern Ireland, Brian Faulkner, argued tenaciously for the merits of internment as a legitimate and effective policy, it soon became clear that it was doomed to failure. A mistaken assumption had been made that the success of internment used against an earlier, much weaker IRA campaign (1956–62) could be repeated again ten years later. Northern Ireland, however, was now a more divided society, one that increasingly became the focus of national and international attention. It was much more difficult to justify such abuses at a time when the voice of civil rights movements had become heard throughout the industrialised world. However, it was at the operational level that the seeds of the failure of internment were sown.

In the years since the end of the IRA's border campaign of the late 1950s, the RUC had failed to update its records on activists and possible suspects. Internment caused irreparable damage to relationships between the Catholic community and the RUC and the army because so many individuals and families were targeted, often on the basis of spurious and inaccurate files. Ironically many of the activists whom the authorities wanted to catch were able to escape by crossing the border into the Irish Republic. Although the use of internment might be viewed as a desperate attempt to bring order to a society increasingly undermined by conflict, it had the opposite effect.

The clear verdict of history is that the great gamble of internment failed. Far from stopping the violence, it immediately produced a ferocious orgy of destruction, a reaction from the Republican communities of sheer rage. In the wider Catholic community the action was presented as a one-sided act in a situation where both communities had their violent men.

(Bloomfield, 1994: 150–1)

Before the introduction of internment 35 people had lost their lives in the first half of 1971. In the second half of 1971, after the introduction of internment, over 150 were killed, almost half of these were Catholics. Twenty-nine of these were shot by soldiers (McKittrick and McVea, 2001: 69). Not only did internment fuel violence, it also had the effect of increasing community support for the Provisional IRA, which had broken away from the Official IRA in 1969 (Taylor, 1997). Talks between the Provisional IRA and the London government, which were aimed at finding a solution to the conflict, were also ended.

Events leading to Bloody Sunday

The slide towards further conflict continued in the six months between the introduction of internment and the events of Bloody Sunday. Street rioting was accompanied by increased paramilitary violence and security force responses to the worsening situation. At the same time of the announcement of internment, a six-month ban was placed on all parades and civil rights marches. The NICRA resolved to defy the ban on demonstrations, and in particular the right to parade in the city centre of Derry.

In the fortnight before Bloody Sunday a number of violent incidents created an atmosphere of tension and fear in the city: '[T]he Provisional IRA had fired 319 rounds at the security forces, killing two soldiers and wounding two others, in 80 shooting incidents in the city; 84 nail bombs had been thrown' (Bardon, 1992: 689). To make matters worse, a march on the internment camp at Magilligan, near Derry, resulted in a confrontation between the army and anti-internment protesters. A significant aspect of the government's action at Magilligan was the use, for the first time, of the

First Battalion of the Parachute Regiment in Derry. This was a 'crack' regiment of the British Army, already recognised for its tough handling of riots and generally loathed by Nationalists in situations elsewhere in Northern Ireland. Although no one was killed, 300 soldiers were used to break up the protest, often using excessive violence. The general climate worsened in the week preceding Bloody Sunday, however, when two policemen were shot dead in Derry and two bombs exploded at the perimeter fence of the Belfast base of the Parachute Regiment.

A number of arguments have been used to explain how and why the Parachute Regiment became involved in this highly contentious situation. Taylor (1997) for example, believes that Bloody Sunday was a 'tragedy waiting to happen' because of the volatile conditions in Derry at the time, although it was difficult to be absolutely sure about what exactly incited the shootings that day. What is apparent in his account, however, was that a consensus had emerged in the British Army establishment that the 'no-go' areas in Derry needed to be challenged and that the local rioters needed to be 'taught a lesson'. The loss of control of much of the city to the IRA following the Battle of the Bogside, alongside the failure of internment, was of obvious concern to the government and rankled with security force personnel. Not only did this create a loss of face for the civil authority and strengthen Unionist complaints that Nationalists were being treated too leniently, but the IRA had used the no-go areas to launch attacks against the police and army. The Parachute Regiment had been used in Belfast to confront other insurgencies, so it appears that they were deemed suitable for this purpose. This interpretation of events, whilst plausible at the time of writing, has been reconsidered in the light of further evidence made available to, and discussed by, a number of other authors.

Of particular interest were the interpretations made in *Eyewitness Bloody Sunday* (Mullan, 1997), which brought into the public domain over 100 eyewitness accounts of the day which were barely considered by the Widgery Tribunal in 1972. On the basis of these accounts it has been suggested not just that the Parachute Regiment acted both recklessly and illegally but that other soldiers on the city walls may have been involved in the shootings. This seminal work led to a series of other publications which question the roles of government ministers and security force personal in ordering the attack. This points towards at worst a conspiracy, at best a series of events which revealed a lack of adequate legal and operational control of army activity, as well as major flaws in the role and operation of the Widgery Tribunal. Walsh's *Bloody Sunday and the Rule of Law in Northern Ireland* (2000) uses Cabinet Office material, and previously hidden statements by soldiers from the Parachute Regiment who carried out the shootings on Bloody Sunday, to construct a convincing argument about systemic failures in the operation, and subsequent alleged cover-ups by military staff. Walsh argues that the events of Bloody Sunday cannot be isolated from a wider, historical malaise in the legal system and body politic of Northern Ireland. Finally, two of the original members of the *Sunday Times* Insight team which gave evidence to the Widgery Tribunal produced a book which describes the events of the day, using declassified documents and new statements from soldiers, civilians and the IRA (Pringle and Jacobson, 2000). This account also reveals a sense of injustice felt by the Derry community, and failure by the state to control its forces.

The immediate events of Bloody Sunday were triggered by an intended march by protesters to Derry city centre on 30 January 1972. It has been estimated that up to 20,000 marchers proceeded towards the city centre where speakers would call for an end to internment. A clash with soldiers was anticipated given the violence at Magilligan and the fact that the march had been made illegal. With the history of trouble the week before at Magilligan, many people, anticipating a riot, decided to go home, satisfied with the size of the turnout. Rioting was a frequent occurrence in Derry during these years, but what was unusual was the degree of violence carried out by the army. There are now a number of accounts that trace the events of the day (McCann, Shiels and Hannigan, 1992; McCafferty, 1989; McClean, 1997; Pringle and Jacobson, 2000; Mullan, 1997; Walsh, 2000). The confrontation between the rioters and army at barrier 14 on William Street and the shootings which wounded Damien Donaghy and John Johnston were to be the first of many violent events of the day. These accounts also record that the army rushed the protestors and chased them to Rossville Flats car park where Jackie Duddy was shot dead. In the Rossville Flats forecourt, three people were shot – Patrick Doherty, Bernard McGuigan and Hugh Gilmore. As the army moved on, Kevin McElhinney, Michael Kelly, Michael McDaid, William Nash and John Young were shot at the rubble barricade in Rossville Street. The final deaths of that day occurred in Glenfadda Park where James Wray, Gerard Donaghy, William McKinney and Gerard McKinney were shot. John Johnston was to die some five months after Bloody Sunday. Many more were injured and traumatised as a result of these events.

Bloody Sunday: the aftermath

Bloody Sunday is, in some respects, one of many traumatic events that have characterised the current Troubles in Northern Ireland. McKittrick and McVea (2001) have estimated that, from 1966 to September 2001, 3,673 people lost their lives. Many tens of thousands more have been physically traumatised (Fay, Morrissey and Smyth, 1999). Although there has been debate about facts surrounding some of the deaths (Fay, Morrissey and Smyth, 1999; McKittrick and McVea, 2001), there is very little dispute about general trends. Over half of all deaths were suffered by civilians, and young men were much more likely to be killed than any other social group. Approximately half of all deaths were caused by Republican paramilitaries and around a third have been attributed to Loyalist paramilitaries. Another one tenth were killed by security forces. Only with the advent of the current peace process is attention at last being paid to the potentially enormous depth of psychological pain and suffering which has occurred over the last 30 years, an issue which is raised in Chapter 7 of this book.

There is an inevitable degree of discomfort in tracing the violent events that followed Bloody Sunday, particularly since space only allows for a broad review of incidents which have caused untold hurt to a large proportion of the population of Northern Ireland, many of whom continue to suffer from such traumas. In the years which have passed there have been a series of incidents which have caused similar multiple deaths and injuries to those which happened on Bloody Sunday (Fay, Morrissey and Smyth, 1999; McKittrick and McVea, 2001; Sutton, 1994). It must also be remembered however, that many more people died as a result of numerous, individual episodes. Each death and injury during this period must have caused incalculable distress to families, friends and communities. It can be argued, however, that Bloody Sunday had a profound political and social impact on Northern Irish society. Not only did it directly lead to the dismantling of the devolved administration at Stormont and the introduction of Direct Rule from Westminster, as an act of state killing, it also marked a watershed in the Troubles. Northern Ireland embarked on a tortuous journey which involved significant inter-communal violence, conflict between the state and paramilitary groups, as well as a series of often failed attempts to address the underlying social and political causes of the violence.

The year that followed Bloody Sunday was by far the most violent of the 30 years of recent conflict in Northern Ireland:

> The 1972 figure of almost 500 killings stands as a vivid illus-tration of the lethal depths to which the troubles descended. There were almost 2,000 explosions and over 10,000 shoot-ing incidents, an average of around 30 shootings per day. Almost 5,000 people were injured. Almost 2,000 armed robberies netted £800,000, most of it going into paramilitary coffers. In the worst month of the entire troubles, July 1972, almost a hundred people died as both Republican and Loyalist groups went on an uninhibited rampage. As the year opened, 17,000 soldiers were available for duty; when it ended, a series of hasty reinforcements had brought the figure to 29,000.
>
> (McKittrick and McVea, 2001: 83)

In the rest of that year, the IRA embarked on a series of bombing attacks, which led to the deaths of seven people at an army base in Aldershot, England, eleven people in a series of explosions around Belfast on Bloody Friday and eight people in an explosion in the county Londonderry village of Claudy. As a result of deteriorating security and virtual collapse of the civil power, the instruments of government were placed in the hands of ministers appointed from the Westminster parliament. Aptly described as 'Direct Rule', this mechanism allowed a Secretary of State for Northern Ireland, and a small number of Ministers of State with responsibilities for numerous portfolios, to govern Northern Ireland. This period lasted from 1972 to 1998 (an exception was a six-month experi-ment involving a power-sharing arrangement between local parties in 1974). The Sunningdale Agreement, which had preceded the establishment of a power-sharing executive in Northern Ireland and all-Ireland institutions in 1974 was, in effect, destroyed by civil unrest that followed industrial action led by workers and Loyalist paramilitaries.

This period in the 1970s saw a rise in sectarian violence often carried out by Loyalists randomly targeting Catholics in vulnerable interface districts in Belfast. In 1974 Loyalist paramilitaries used car bombs to kill 22 people in Dublin and five civilians in Monaghan (three died later of their injuries). Later in the year the IRA used bombs to kill five people in Guildford and 21 in Birmingham. The Ulster Volunteer Force (UVF), a Loyalist paramilitary group, was involved in a range of atrocities in 1975, including the Miami Showband killings. These were followed by a series of attacks in October when twelve died, including four UVF men. In 1976 ten people died in the Kingsmill massacre and in early 1976 twelve people died in the La Mon hotel bombing. In 1979 18 soldiers and one civilian were blown up by a bomb laid by the IRA in Warrenpoint. Also in 1979 nine RUC officers lost their lives as the result of an IRA mortar bomb attack on their station in Newry.

After a relative lull in violence towards the end of the 1970s, the hunger strikes of 1981 led to the death of ten Republicans, followed in 1982 by bombs in London that killed eleven soldiers and the later deaths of three civilians. Towards the end of that year 17 people died in an explosion in Ballykelly. A year later five people died in a bomb in Harrods, London, and in 1984 five people were killed by an IRA bomb at the Conservative Party Conference in Brighton. Arguably the next most significant attempt to change constitutional arrangements took place with the signing of the Anglo-Irish Agreement between the British and Irish governments in 1985. For the first time since partition, the government of the Republic of Ireland was given a degree of input into the policy-making processes of Northern Ireland (Hadden, Rutherford and Merrette, 1989). This step, however, failed to stem the flow of violence. Eight members of the IRA and one civilian were killed by the SAS (Special Air Services) in Loughgall in 1987, and later in the year eleven people died following the Enniskillen Poppy Day bombing. In 1988 eight people, including members of the IRA, civilians and soldiers were killed in a series of events that followed an SAS attack in Gibraltar.

In the summer of that year 14 soldiers and three IRA members lost their lives in separate incidents. A year later eleven soldiers were killed in an IRA explosion in Kent.

Although deaths in the Troubles had fallen steadily from the peak of 1972, nine soldiers were killed in two incidents in 1990. In early 1992 nine civilians died as a result of the Teeban massacre, five were shot dead in a bookies shop in Belfast and four IRA men lost their lives in the space of one month. A number of violent events led up to the ceasefires of 1994. In March of 1993 two children died in an explosion in Warrington, England and four civilian workers were killed in Castlerock. Later that year nine people died in a bomb explosion on the Shankill Road in Belfast and seven in the village of Greysteel. Six people lost their lives in a random shooting attack in another village, Loughinisland, in the summer of 1994.

The inter party talks that led eventually to the Belfast Agreement (NIO, 1998a) provided a structure in which a power-sharing executive, a north–south body and a body representing the islands of Britain and Ireland were formed. Arguably this is the most significant constitutional development since the partition of Ireland. These sets of political and administrative processes seemed to offer the greatest opportunity in a generation for resolving deep-seated grievances that have fuelled decades of violence. Despite this optimism, two atrocities seemed to affect public opinion and the political process in the years that followed the signing of the Belfast Agreement. Three young brothers died in a petrol bomb attack in Ballymoney in 1998, and 29 people and two unborn children lost their lives in the Real IRA bombing of the centre of Omagh just over a month later.

Northern Ireland post-Belfast Agreement

It can be argued that a defining moment in the path towards conflict resolution was the signing of the Belfast Agreement. In the seven years between 1998 and 2005 the Agreement has partially fulfilled the expectations of the majority of people, both sides of the Irish border, who voted for it. Improving relationships between the UK and Irish Republic governments, the establishment of a regional Assembly at Stormont, and an expanded number of cross-border bodies suggest that society and politics in Northern Ireland is gradually moving away from the preoccupation with conflict and blame and looking towards reconciliation both within and outside. Yet this process has not been without its problems. For example the Assembly has been suspended on a number of occasions because of Unionist concerns that the IRA has not been committed to disarmament. Sinn Fein, for its part, has argued that it has adhered to the letter of the Agreement and brought the Republican movement along with it. Although there has been a considerable reduction in British Army activity and the RUC has been replaced by the Police Service of Northern Ireland (PSNI), Republicans tend to assert that the state apparatus is a threat to their constituency. Many Unionists, on the other hand, view continuing paramilitary violence and illegal activity as evidence of bad faith on the part of the Republican movement and Loyalist paramilitary groups. In the Assembly elections of 2003 the Democratic Unionist Party (DUP) and Sinn Fein became the two biggest parties and, in effect, hold the key to negotiations through such political impasses. Talks between these parties and the two governments were set back by allegations that the IRA was involved in the biggest bank robbery in the United Kingdom, which took place in Belfast just before Christmas 2004.

Despite these problems, there is a perception that Northern Irish society is in a state of movement and transformation, at least partly created as a consequence of the negotiated settlement described above. The economy has grown and there are many signs of prosperity in terms of employment, disposable income, private housing, business development and tourist visitor numbers. Yet the deep-seated effects of three decades of conflict are a constant reminder of how far there is to travel in terms of peace building. Following the Belfast Agreement prisoners convicted of scheduled offences and attracting a sentence of five years or more became eligible to apply for early release to the Independent Sentence Review Commissioners. Between 1993 and 2002 there were 357 life sentence prisoners released on license from prison in Northern Ireland (NIO, 2003: www.nio.gov.uk/ digestinfo.pdf). At the same time the state and other parties have sought to address the problems raised by victims and survivors of 35 years of the Troubles. This issue is discussed and analysed in

Chapter 7. Although the numbers of people being killed as a direct result of the Troubles has dropped to single figures per annum during this period, concern has been regularly expressed about what has been described as continuing 'low-level violence' often carried out by Loyalist and Republican paramilitaries against their own communities. These often involve beatings on young people involved in offending behaviour in communities where the PSNI are not trusted. Many Republicans, for their part, point to a continuing failure of the state to address security force reforms and mechanisms to address past human rights injustices by the state.

Summary

The events of Bloody Sunday cannot be viewed in isolation from a range of historical, social, political and economic factors presented in this chapter. Bloody Sunday occurred at a moment of crisis in the state, compounded by substantial faults in key decisions made by the authorities and individuals on the day. What flowed from this tragic event was a dramatic escalation of violence, which affected not just Northern Ireland, but also Britain and the Republic of Ireland. This is a crucial context for understanding some of the reasons why Bloody Sunday happened and how this, and subsequent events, left an indelible mark on the lives of those who lost relatives on the day. Yet there is a perception that the Belfast Agreement and its complex set of political and social arrangements have delivered positive gains for this society. In the chapter which follows we review this history, but from a different perspective – using a critical analysis of state violence.

2 Perspectives on state violence

In Chapter 1 we traced events that led to, and followed on from, Bloody Sunday. There seems little doubt that Bloody Sunday had a profound effect on the trajectory of violence in the following years. We argue in this chapter that there are some features of the event on Bloody Sunday which differentiates it from many other terrible acts of violence during the years of the Troubles. A particular feature of this tragedy was that the deaths and injuries that occurred were at the hands of the state. In what follows a context will be provided which seeks to explain the historical, social and political contexts that led to state violence on the day. The chapter begins with a discussion about ways of defining state violence, using international illustrations, before going on to analyse the history of state violence in Northern Ireland. In conclusion we argue that a critical understanding of the nature of state violence is crucial in understanding how trauma resolution might occur for families of people killed on Bloody Sunday, and others who have suffered similar losses.

Defining state violence

The violence of the state has been an ever-present aspect of modern history, but it is the rise of the nation state and the intensity and frequency of war and conflict in the twentieth century which highlights the destructive capacity that institutions of state possess. The more visible actions of state power and violence during the two world wars have in some way been replaced by a more pervasive, but often hidden, role in international and national conflicts. These developments have coincided with the increased use of technology to assert and develop systems of state power. Even if it was possible to quantify such activity, problems remain about how violence for and against the state is defined and presented. A conventional solution to this conundrum is to classify state violence as 'force', legitimised through the political process and systems of governance. Of course the degree to which the state's power is legitimised varies with time and is differentiated according to how different social groupings perceive the validity of the state's mandate. The way in which the state was formed and developed in Northern Ireland illustrates these points. A substantial minority of the population has always questioned the authority of the state; this situation was further compounded by the fact that the political system tended to be insensitive to minority rights. Confidence will also be eroded if and when the state, and its actors, uses violence indiscriminately or disproportionately. Again this can be said to have happened in the case of Northern Ireland, and is a theme which is developed below.

It is crucial for the state to maintain this monopoly of power and legitimacy, and to challenge those individuals and groups who disagree with its position. If political processes are perceived to be representative, and a consensus exists in civil society that policies are just, then this task becomes easier. Problems arise when these democratic building blocks are not in place, or are unstable.

There are numerous contemporary examples of state violence throughout the world and in different types of regimes, both liberal democratic and authoritarian. Perhaps the most startling example of state violence in a western liberal democratic state is the increased use of the death penalty in many jurisdictions in the United States. For example, in 2003 65 people were executed, bringing the total since this form of state killing was reintroduced in 1976 to 885. People from ethnic minority communities are highly over represented in these statistics, and there is a particular international concern about the execution of minors under the age of 18 (Amnesty International, 2004).

The breadth and volume of state violence throughout the world is extensive, even given the probability that underestimation takes place. Extralegal forms of state violence – those which take place without justification or are legitimised by the laws of the state which is conducting the violence – are widespread. Iadicola and Shupa (2003) describe the characteristics and variety of state violence, whether administered internally on subject populations or externally in international contexts. Types of state violence include war, genocide, assassination, torture, experiments, propaganda campaigns, and the use of agents provocateurs. Many of these violations remain uncovered, for example the use of routine abuses of human rights in Latin America (Munck, 2000: 6–8; Hamber, 1997) whereas some, like genocide, continue even when known to the international community (Campbell, 2001: 53). There is a long history of such violence for example in the case of the Holocaust, and in Cambodia, Rwanda, Bosnia and Darfur. Specific social and political groups tend to be the targets of state violence – indigenous and ethnic minority groups, dissident political groups, women, children and peasants. Some of these groups may be involved in insurgency against the state or simply become victims of direct or indirect violence against marginalised and powerless sections of society.

A variety of agents carry out state violence (Iadicola and Shupa, 2003), ranging from military or government forces and national and international secret police, to the less tangible, but more sinister political or private groups that are organised and sponsored by the state. It is also important to acknowledge that regimes can be differentiated by the levels of brutality which they inflict on their own and other's populations, often this can be judged in relation to weak experiences of democracy and legal safeguards against human rights abuses. However, very few nations, across all continents, escape the criticism that such violence occurs in the majority of cases (Amnesty International, 2004).

Single incidents of state violence are sometimes captured forever in the international consciousness, whereas others, tragically, are never to be discovered and left trapped in history. Two events, which bear some similarities to Bloody Sunday but which occurred in quite different social and political contexts reveal this sense of loss of legitimacy in the political regime. They are also examples of how loss, grief and trauma remain for survivors, decades after the events. These are the Sharpeville Massacre in South Africa and the Kent State University killings in the United States.

On 21 March 1960, 69 people were killed and many others injured when the South African police opened fire on those protesting against the pass laws, in the township of Sharpeville in the Transvaal. The event signalled the start of concerted armed resistance in South Africa, and prompted worldwide condemnation of South Africa's Apartheid policies. No policemen were charged over the killings, nor was there any substantive official investigation into the events until the Truth and Reconciliation Commission some 38 years later. It found that the police failed to give the crowd an order to disperse and that they continued to fire, shooting many people in the back as they fled. The state security forces made little or no attempt to coordinate or provide medical attention for those who were subsequently wounded. Many of these protesting were apolitical and women and children. There is no evidence that any of these were armed. The Truth and Reconciliation Commission found the former state and the minister of police directly responsible for gross human rights violations (Truth and Reconciliation Commission of South Africa, 1998).

The Kent State University killings (Gordon, 1995) occurred after students protested about the decision by the US government to bomb Cambodia in 1970. On 4 May 1970 the National Guard fired directly into demonstrating students, injuring 13 and killing four. None of the guardsmen admitted responsibility for firing at the unarmed students, nor were they later punished, civilly, administratively or criminally. It has subsequently not been possible to establish the truth of this event; most of the guardsmen were unidentifiable because they were wearing gas masks and had removed their name tags. No ballistic tests were carried out after the event and accusations by the state that a sniper was present remain unproven because of the absence of eyewitness or photographic evidence to support this claim. No investigation took place about the killings, but a criminal trial followed which was marked by a perception amongst commentators that the presiding judge favoured the evidence of defendants. A civil suit brought by the parents of those who were killed and wounded was undermined by evidence presented by the plaintiffs' lawyers. These factors at least partly explain why, at the original trial, the jury returned a verdict for the defendants, although this verdict was overturned on appeal because the original judge did not take seriously enough the attempted coercion of a juror. On the eve of the appeal trial the plaintiffs settled with the state for $675,000, which was divided 13 ways. Half of it went to the most seriously wounded survivor, and only $15,000 went to the other families who had lost their children.

Some parallels can be drawn between these two examples of state violence and the events which surrounded Bloody Sunday. The victims were protesting against perceived injustices and became subject to disproportionate state violence. Subsequent inquiries revealed uncontrolled and illegitimate state force, and there appeared to be an absence of resolution for families and those who were injured. The fact that the state was the source of this violation is a crucial issue which we will return to later in this and other chapters.

Despite the fact that there is ample evidence of many acts of state violence throughout the world, predominant discourses about the causes of political and social violence tend to favour the world view of dominant states and interests. It could be argued that now, as we enter the twenty-first century, in particular after the bombing of the World Trade Center in New York on 9/11, this issue is at the centre of local, national and world politics. The essential message which has emerged from this tragedy is that the world should be fearful of terrorist violence, and that democratic states should take a more robust view on policies which will defend nations and eliminate this threat. This, it has been asserted by political leaders, necessarily implies a reappraisal of the state's commitment to principles of human rights. Yet if we take a step back in history it is possible to view this development in terms of an uneven process of western state activity, particularly in the period after the Second World War. Most notably, counter-insurgency methods were concentrated on finding ways of dealing with Nationalist violence in former European colonies, and latterly by the United States during the war in Vietnam and south-east Asia. The conflicts in the Middle East, and Central and Southern America became included in such analyses.

It was not long before counter-insurgency thought was applied to terrorism in Europe during the 1970s and 1980s, before the events of 9/11 in New York led to an outpouring of literature on the subject (Scratton, 2002). Although there is a great deal of variation in these accounts, in terms of cultural context, sophistication of analysis and competing political ideologies, it is possible to discern common threads which run through the genre (Coulter, 1999; Campbell, 1986). A fundamental starting point is that violence is largely the prerogative of the terrorist; the corollary is that the state is required to use force to counter the insurgency. A working assumption is that violence against the state is carried out by unrepresentative cliques, and often this activity is also associated with individual or group psychopathology. This representation of political violence, however, is partial and oblique, and hardly stands thorough examination. There is little doubt that terrorist groups have carried out profoundly violent acts, often against innocents and without remorse, but these acts are rarely driven by reason of individual immorality or madness. Invariably there is some form of explanatory framework available which can help critically analyse the social, economic and political backdrop to the activities of insurgents. The same level of critical thinking should be applied to state violence, which is often emasculated, hidden from view by government rhetoric and reinforced by popular discourses on the causes of conflict. In doing so it is possible to begin to reveal the nature and degree of state violence:

> If terrorism means political intimidation by violence or its threats, and if we allow the definition to include violence by states and agents of violence, then we find that the major form of terrorism in the world today is that practised by states and their agents and allies, and that, quantitatively, anti-state terrorism pales into relative insignificance in comparison to it.
> (Chomsky and Herman (1979) in Sukla, 2000: 1)

There is, however, plenty of evidence to suggest that the state is consistently involved in violence against its citizens across a wide spectrum of circumstances. Even where there is a degree of popular consensus about the role of the state in society, the distinction between force and violence can often become blurred. At times of internal crisis, or changes forced by political and social pressures, the adverse power of the state becomes manifest. A more detailed account of these processes with reference to the specific example of Northern Ireland will now be presented.

State violence in Northern Ireland, 1921–98

As we alluded to in Chapter 1, any discussion of state violence in Northern Ireland must take into account the historical context which led to partition and subsequent problems faced by the state over the following 80 years. Political violence, both carried out against the state and by the state in response to the insurgency, was an intermittent feature of the decades which preceded the current Troubles. The perception that the state was threatened both internally and externally led the Unionist administration to use exceptional powers as part of its security apparatus: 'Any analysis of Northern Ireland's legal history informs us that this is a state which has never known anything but emergency rule' (Ni Aolain, 2000: 22). For example, from 1928 to 1971 the Special Powers Act allowed for the use of internment without trial, retro-spective criminal legislation and search without warrant. It has been argued that this continuous state of emergency seriously compromised the assumption that Northern Ireland, as a part of the United Kingdom, could be described as a liberal democratic entity. What made matters worse was that these laws were almost always applied to the minority Nationalist population, sometimes based on faulty intelligence or inadequate evidence. Thus, in 1922 the Special Powers Act was used to intern 500 members of Sinn Fein and their sympathisers and in 1938 827 men were interned (Ni Aolain, 2000: 27). In the post-war period these powers were also used sporadically at times of heightened IRA activity. The unequal application of such emergency laws was compounded by the fact that the security forces increasingly became drawn from the unionist community. In 1921 21 per cent of the Royal Ulster Constabulary were Catholics, this dropped to 17 per cent by 1931 and 11 per cent at the start of the present Troubles in 1969, and 8 per cent by the mid-1990s (Hillyard, 1997: 105). This decline in minority representation was probably the result of a combination of factors, including paramilitary intimidation of recruits and a lack of Nationalist confidence in the forces of law and order.

It was, however, the dramatic escalation of violence, firstly by protesters and the state, and latterly paramilitaries in the late 1960s and early 1970s which brought these contentious issues to national and international audiences. As in previous crises within the state the justification for repressive forms of law and order was the sense of threat to the social, economic and political fabric of the state; when one examines the levels of anti-state violence over the 30 years of conflict, it is possible to understand some of the concerns of politicians and policy makers. During peak years of the Troubles in the 1970s hundreds of people lost their lives or were badly injured and traumatised by incidents mostly carried out by paramilitary groups. When the causes of Troubles-related deaths are analysed (Fay, Morrissey and Smyth, 1999; McKittrick and McVea, 2001) Republican paramilitaries have been complicit in over half, and Loyalist paramilitaries in nearly one third, of all of those killed in the last three decades. State violence, on the other hand, only accounts for about 10 per cent of all deaths; why then should some commentators take such a critical view of the role of the state in the conflict? As we have suggested above, when the state becomes involved in the killing and injuring of its citizens, or withdrawing their civil rights, the notional contract between individuals and their government is eroded, leading to distrust and a potential further cycle of violence. Rolston (2000), in his anthology of victims' stories of state violence in Northern Ireland, suggests the following distinctions between those who suffer because of the actions of the state, and those who have been traumatised by other actors in this conflict:

> My focus is not on all victims, but solely on those killed by the state. There are two main reasons for this: firstly they are qualitatively different from other killings because they have been carried out by an institution which, uniquely, claims to protect all citizens; and second, these victims have often been forgotten in the past, whilst those who have sought to keep the memory alive have been marginalized by the state and its institutions. None of this is to insinuate that the suffering of other victims and their relatives is necessarily any less than those killed by the state even if in recent years some groups have had a more sympathetic hearing.
>
> (Rolston, 2000: xiii)

Of the 10 per cent of people killed by the state during the period 1969 up to the Belfast Agreement in 1998, about 80 per cent of these were killed by the British Army and around 15 per cent by the RUC. Most of these took place in the early years of the Troubles – in 1972 alone 83 people died. Over 50 per cent of those who were killed by security forces during the three decades of the Troubles were civilians, with the large majority of these (83 per cent) being Catholics. Republicans accounted for 37 per cent of these deaths and only 4 per cent were Loyalists (Rolston, 2000). A number of attempts have been made to classify types of state violence in Northern Ireland during this period. For example Hillyard (1997: 106) describes the characteristics of the security apparatus which varied according to events on the ground and the vicissitudes of local, national and international politics. The mechanisms which the state used included: an alleged 'shoot to kill' policy, the use of live and baton rounds, strategies of stop and search and detention, ill-treatment in custody, prolonged detention, the use of informers, collusion with Loyalist paramilitaries, the intimidation of lawyers, strip searching and the transfer of prisoners to British jails. Some allegations of ill-treatment and the misuse of emergency powers were subsequently criticised by the European Commission, the International Court of Human Rights and Amnesty International.

Ni Aolain (2000) divides the Troubles into three phases of state security activity. The first period between 1969–74 is described as the 'militarisation phase' which plots the arrival of the army. This consisted of a brief 'honeymoon period' of relative calm and acceptance by both communities, but which was quickly replaced by escalating conflict, between the security forces and the Nationalist populations of Belfast and Derry. Soon the security forces were engaged with the IRA and latterly Loyalist paramilitaries. The disintegration of political and civil authority led to a situation of emergency and military primacy – the army killed 90 per cent of those who died in these extremely violent early years of the Troubles, and many of these deaths occurred in riot and cross-fire situations.

The second phase (1975–80) Ni Aolain describes as one of 'normalisation'. The failed policy of internment which was introduced in 1971 was replaced by an attempt to use the law to criminalise political violence. The intensity of the IRA bombing and the nascent threat of Loyalist paramilitary violence led to increased responses by the new government, now directed from Westminster. A range of laws replaced the Special Powers Act (Hillyard, 1997). The Emergency Provisions Act (1973) introduced a separate legal system for 'political' offences which included the abolition of trial by jury, the introduction of special rules for the admissibility of certain evidence and the crime of membership of proscribed organisations. The Prevention of Terrorism Act (1974) allowed for port controls, extended powers of arrest, exclusion orders, new criminal offences and the proscription of certain organisations. Ni Aolain argues that the use of state force became less necessary because the police increasingly regained civil and peacekeeping powers, the military were more careful in abiding by rules of engagement and the law, and the courts were relatively successful in processing paramilitary offences.

Phase three (1981–94) is described in terms of the prevailing use by the state of 'counter-insurgency and extraordinary law'. Directly after the hunger strikes of 1980–81 the police temporarily engaged in counter-insurgency measures, including a controversial shoot to kill policy. Intense international criticism of this strategy, and ultimate failure of the uses of 'supergrasses' (where the state uses key witnesses to testify against defendants) in courts, led to the re-establishment of the military's position in a prime counter-insurgency role. The use of 'set-piece', planned confrontations with paramilitaries who were allegedly carrying out acts of violence, usually involved undercover units such as the Special Air Services (SAS) using lethal force. In this period, 40 paramilitaries (29 armed) were killed in set-piece incidents, most of whom were IRA members. Throughout the 1980s and early 1990s concern was also expressed about how the state allegedly used Loyalist paramilitaries to carry out assassinations both against Nationalists and Republicans.

In 2004 the British government announced its intention to carry out individual inquiries into the role of the state and others in the deaths of four people, where collusion was suspected. This flowed from recommendations made by Judge Cory who was earlier appointed to examine these cases. Two of these were solicitors (Pat Finucane and Rosemary Nelson) whose murders were probably carried out by Loyalist paramilitaries. One was a Loyalist prisoner (Billy Wright) killed by Republicans whilst in jail. Finally Robert Hamill, a Catholic man, was killed by a group of men whilst an RUC vehicle was parked close by. Although each of these cases varies considerably, the allegations are that the state had a role to play in the deaths, either by collusion with Loyalist paramilitaries, or by a conscious decision not to act when lives would have been saved. It remains to be seen whether any of the families involved will accept the terms and conditions of these inquiries and their subsequent findings.

It is apparent from this account of the history of the use of state violence and extraordinary powers in Northern Ireland that these activities have been shaped by a range of factors including political instability, the constant threat of violence and insurgency and the relative lack of the sort of accountability for security force measures which one would expect in a liberal democracy. As the years and decades have gone by many individuals, families and communities have suffered, often with lack of recourse to due process and the resolution of their grief. Fundamental questions remain for this society about the way in which violence has affected the well being of all citizens. For this particular section of society, those who have been harmed by the state, many of these issues remain to be addressed.

Reforming the state and the resolution of conflict: Northern Ireland post-Belfast Agreement

The paramilitary ceasefires of 1994 and the political events which led to the signing of the Belfast Agreement in 1998 marked a watershed in the conflict and raised hopes about how past injustices might be resolved. The Agreement, and the range of policy initiatives which flowed from it, has put in place a number of strategies which may lead to the democratisation of the political system and redress the harm caused by the activities of the state and paramilitaries. As we have discussed above, the inadequacy and misuse of the law, combined with the sometimes unsustainable use of state violence against sections of the community in Northern Ireland have left a legacy of mistrust which will be hard to resolve. As Walsh puts it in the context of the events of Bloody Sunday:

> One of the most disturbing aspects of Bloody Sunday ... is the dismal failure of the law and the legal system to prevent the killings and woundings from happening in the first place and to deliver justice to the victims and the broader community after the event.
>
> (Walsh, 2000: 304)

There seems little doubt that the resolution of these and other events must take place in the social and political environments which might emerge from the Belfast Agreement (Maginnity and Darby, 2002; Walsh, 2000; Ni Aolain, 2000). Some tentative steps towards such change have already been taken. Political agreement has led to a three-strand approach to resolving long-standing historical problems which have bedevilled progress in Northern Ireland. This includes a power-sharing arrangement between Unionists, Nationalists and Republicans in a devolved assembly, as well as political and ministerial links between the north and south of Ireland, and Britain and Ireland. The state has invested in programmes to assist victims and survivors of the Troubles (an issue which is further discussed in Chapter 7) and reformed the police force. The Northern Ireland Human Rights Commission has been established to examine existing and future laws, many of which adversely affected citizens in the past.

How then might these changes affect the experiences of those who have suffered at the hands of the state? At the human level there are countless stories of grief and resentment which followed the violent events of the past 30 years which affected civilians, members of the security forces and paramilitary groups, and which remain to be resolved. For those who have been killed or injured by the state, the experience may be different, although no less painful than others. Rolston (2000) suggests that, in the past, their voices are less likely to be heard against the more powerful versions of events portrayed by the state, sometimes leading to misrepresentation and vilification of victims' accounts. The manipulation of information and images is a central feature of many states' counter-insurgency strategies both in Northern Ireland and throughout the world (Coulter, 1999).

Rolston argues that families of those who have been killed experience common obstacles to resolution, because of failures in the legal system, harassment by security forces and feelings of guilt by association. Respondents suggested a variety of mechanisms, legal and otherwise, which might lead to resolution of grief and loss and a sense of injustice. Some wanted those who killed their family member to be prosecuted so that due process would officially record the injustice and the appropriate retribution would be administered. Others were less concerned with

[36]

individual prosecutions but focused instead on the need to expose those in high office who colluded in the killings. Rolston points out that all saw the need for the truth to be revealed, through whichever mechanisms may be available, including a possible truth and reconciliation commission or individual judicial inquiries in specific cases.

Summary

This chapter began by exploring the complex, ideological nature of debates on state violence which have become even more contested following the events of 9/11. We have argued that popular discourses about the legitimacy of state activity, either locally or internationally, should be critically analysed. This is crucial if a more adequate explanation about the power of the state and its capacity to inflict violence on its citizens is to be understood. The case of Northern Ireland illustrates how a sense of legitimacy about the role of the state was not evident for many citizens, and still remains a problem, despite the reforms of the last decade. Where the state has been explicitly involved in killing and injuring sections of the population, many unresolved issues of grief and injustice inevitably remain. In Chapters 1 and 2 we have briefly highlighted key themes in the history of Northern Ireland, the violence which occurred over the last 30 years, and the role of the state in either managing, prolonging or resolving the conflict. These themes will prepare the ground for the chapters which follow. These report the views of family members who suffered as a result of Bloody Sunday and explore how the state is seeking to deal with these traumas.

3 Posttraumatic Stress Disorder, grief, mourning and healing

The concept of Posttraumatic Stress Disorder (PTSD) provides the framework in this text for understanding the responses of Bloody Sunday family members to the events of 30 January 1972. Data that emerged from interviews with family members indicated that PTSD symptomatology was evident for many of them. In the following discussion we critically review the evolution of the PTSD concept from the First World War to the present day. As we explore the concept, we provide an explanation for widely varying responses to trauma and present perspectives on grief and mourning, the interaction between grief and trauma, and the role of storytelling in promoting healing. We argue that Type 2 or a continuous form of trauma might be an appropriate concept to apply to the circumstances of the families.

The history of the concept of PTSD

Among the many competing ideas that have been used to explain the impact of violence on the psychological well being of victims, PTSD has achieved predominance, particularly in the United States. The term was first used in the third edition of the *Diagnostic and Statistical Manual of Mental Disorders (DSM III)* of the American Psychiatric Association in 1980. As early as the First World War a syndrome was recognised in battlefield situations and referred to with labels such as 'irritable heart of the soldier', 'shell shock', or 'combat neurosis' (Gersons and Carlier, 1992). All these terms connote some type of illness or psychological defect such as fragments of shells in people's heads, a neurosis with childhood antecedents, or an inherent weakness in people suffering from the disorder. 'Shell shock' was epidemic in the First World War with hundreds of thousands afflicted. Exasperated generals sought a quick solution to a complex psychological experience by executing victims for cowardice. Psychiatrists tended to label the syndrome as 'hysteria' and generally dismissed the possibility of long-term implications. As a result of inadequate treatment, thousands who survived the war remained in psychiatric hospitals for the rest of their lives (Stone, 1985).

During the war, the French psychologist C. S. Myers responded to the military need to return soldiers quickly to the front lines. He used hypnosis to provide the affected soldiers with an opportunity for catharsis of painful, repressed emotions, and met with enough success to enable some soldiers to return to duty. His work, however, reinforced the notion that 'shell shock' was related to early childhood experiences, conflicts, fears, and defences against destructive impulses. From this perspective, trauma was considered to be the consequence of inner neurotic conflict and this served as a basis for therapy (Gersons and Carlier, 1992).

The prevalence of war trauma after the First and Second World Wars eventually led to major changes in the delivery of mental health services and to a better understanding of the human response to horrific events. Interest in traumatic psychological disorders after the Second World War was not just confined to combat-related trauma. The increasing awareness of psychological trauma in the civilian population led to interest in studying a variety of traumatic situations and experiences. Lindemann (1944) identified a cluster of responses, now recognised as PTSD, which he called 'acute grief syndrome' among previously healthy friends and relatives of people who had died in the Coconut Grove nightclub fire disaster in Boston, Massachusetts. In developing a therapeutic response to trauma, practitioners increasingly found an acute event rather than details of a person's past to be the starting point for therapy.

The PTSD concept has received a great deal of attention in the United States, especially in research related to the treatment of Vietnam War veterans, victims of rape and childhood sexual abuse (Herman, 1992). More recently the concept has been used in the United Kingdom to explore trauma related to the Falklands War, the Northern Ireland Troubles, civil disasters and the long-term effects of the Second World War on veterans and civilians (Bell et al., 1988; Davies, 1997; Dorahy et al., 2003; Gibson, 1996; Gillespie et al., 2002; Hunt, 1997; Loughrey et al., 1988; Luce et al., 2002; McGarvey and Collins, 2001; Orner, 1997; Shevlin and McGuigan, 2003; Waugh, 1997).

The *DSM-III* (1980) defined PTSD for the first time as a normal human reaction to an extremely traumatic event. The syndrome appears to be a serious, commonly occurring problem (deVries, 1996; Gersons and Carlier, 1992; Roth and Lebowitz, 1988), and PTSD is now considered to be an acquired disorder that impairs functioning (van der Kolk and van der Hart 1991; van der Kolk 1994; van der Kolk and Fisler, 1995).

PTSD represents a collection of responses and symptoms following a psychologically distressing event that is outside the range of ordinary, tolerable human experiences (American Psychiatric Association, 1994). The syndrome may be the result of being intentionally harmed or being exposed to the grotesque, such as horribly maimed bodies after an accident, suddenly losing a loved one in a violent manner, particularly if the survivor witnessed the death, or being informed of such an event. Other precipitants of PTSD include learning that one has been exposed to poisons, deadly chemicals or radiation, or has caused death, severe injury or harm to another (Green, 1993). Such an event would be extremely distressing to anyone, and is associated with fear, terror, helplessness, and inability to escape or to take action to influence the outcome. Such experiences overwhelm ordinary human defences and may produce significant and prolonged changes, both physical and emotional. Responses include persistent expectation of danger, intrusions or the involuntary re-experiencing of the ingrained traumatic moment, and constriction, a numbing response to powerlessness. According to the *DSM-IV* (American Psychiatric Association, 1994: 424–9), PTSD is characterised by the following:

- behavioural reactions to the event that is being relived, not present circumstances
- numbing of responsiveness, detachment, or estrangement from other people
- decreased interest in activities previously enjoyed
- loss of intimacy, tenderness, and sexuality
- heightened awareness and hyper-alertness
- sleep disturbances with nightmares, sleeplessness, early morning awakening and insomnia
- survivor guilt, with doubt and self-blame

- trouble concentrating, memory impairment, and a sense of unreality that may persist for weeks or months
- phobic avoidance, fear of being alone or of going near the place where the trauma occurred
- reminders of the event provoke strong emotional reactions
- a sense of foreshortened life span.

Herman (1992) contended that the degree of trauma experienced depends upon whether the trauma originated from a natural event as opposed to a horrific event created by humans. She asserted that trauma due to human-made catastrophe is much more severe. If the trauma stems from a natural phenomenon, it is a disaster; if created by humankind, it is an atrocity.

Victims sometimes wait years before disclosing traumatic events. They come to the attention of health and social care workers because of life difficulties and problems associated with psychological defences common with PTSD. Those affected may rely on alcohol and other substances as a way of coping, and often see themselves as powerless and betrayed. This is particularly the case if the perpetrator of the trauma was one's father or other caretaker in a position of control (Roth and Lebowitz, 1988). A fundamental injustice has occurred and basic trust was shattered. This requires a resolution that will restore some sense of justice (Herman, 1992; Stallard and Law, 1994). The strategies involved in treatment and healing include provision of safety, remembrance and mourning, regaining a sense of power and control in one's life, membership of support groups, and attempts to bring offenders to justice or other related social advocacy (Gibson, 1996; Herman, 1992).

We have observed that the Bloody Sunday family members who told their stories for this book exhibited a full array of the sequelae of trauma which stemmed from the time they heard the news about the violent death of their relatives, or actually witnessed violence that day, and compounded thereafter by a profound sense of betrayal by the state. After years of silent suffering and attempts to cope with psychological pain with defence mechanisms such as repression and numbing, often facilitated by Valium and/or alcohol, many family members embraced the Bloody Sunday Justice Campaign as a means of seeking trauma resolution.

Biological perspectives and PTSD

Pierre Janet (1920) hypothesised that traumatic events are etched in the mind and serve to torment the victim who repeatedly returns to the traumatic memory and re-experiences it. He argued that horrific events and the associated emotional responses experienced by the person during the trauma interfere with proper processing of the information related to the event. This in turn leads to the development of distressing symptoms. These include psychologically re-living the event, amnesia about the event, and hyper-responsiveness to stimuli such as loud noises which produce intense reactions. Contemporary researchers (van der Kolk and van der Hart, 1991; van der Kolk, 1994; van der Kolk and Fisler, 1995) expanded Janet's work and proposed a biochemical explanation for the PTSD syndrome. Most memories are altered by the passage of time and affected by the context of life experiences. Some memories, particularly traumatic memories, can become fixed and unalterable despite the passage of time, and are not assimilated into a coherent understanding of life experiences. Traumatised individuals re-experience these memories through intrusions. The behaviours and symptoms of those with PTSD are attributed to changes that occur in the neurological system as the trauma is experienced. The basis for nightmares, flashbacks, and physical sensations are found in the abnormal functioning of portions of the limbic system of the brain and the autonomic nervous system. These systems play important roles in preserving the individual at times of life-threatening stress. Ironically, for trauma victims, these life preserving biochemical responses contribute to the indelibility of the traumatic memory and associated symptoms, particularly if the person was rendered helpless and unable to respond at the time. The individual is left in a constant state of 'fight or flight' and the body responds accordingly, out of proportion to what may actually be occurring at the moment.

Type 1 and Type 2 traumas

Many Bloody Sunday family members unquestionably suffered a severe trauma the day their relative was killed. The effects of that day linger in serious and pernicious ways. A casual observer may wonder why family members continue to experience severe symptoms, why they have not recovered, grieved their dead and moved on with their lives. The traumatic event, after all, occurred more than 30 years ago. We believe that an explanation for the long-standing, unresolved trauma can be found by distinguishing between types of trauma and the responses they evoke (Terr, 1990).

A Type 1 trauma may arise from a single unexpected event, such as a natural disaster, car accident or a sexual assault. Victims typically experience an acute, short-term posttraumatic response, but they tend to recover in a timely fashion with a good prognosis. It is important to note that not everyone who experiences symptoms of posttraumatic stress is destined to develop PTSD. Personality variables, a person's appraisal of the trauma, prior traumatic experiences, cultural factors, capacity to use social supports and primary responsibility for the care of others impact on how individuals respond (Hunt, 1997). Most people are able to 'work through' using their own resources and the support of others (deVries 1996; McFarlane, 1996).

In sharp contrast, when a Type 2 trauma occurs, it is usually deliberate and human-made. Populations suffering from the effects of a Type 2 trauma endure ongoing physical or sexual abuse. They may be involved in hostage situations, be soldiers in combat or civilians living in a war zone. The response to this type of trauma produces PTSD symptoms, which are chronic, long-standing and associated with co-morbid features such as chronic depression and anxiety, substance abuse and physical ill-health. Victims may develop an altered view of the self and the world accompanied by mistrust and feelings of guilt, shame and worthlessness. This may lead to long-standing interpersonal problems and to a complex PTSD reaction (Herman, 1992).

The events of Bloody Sunday constitute a single trauma; however, subsequent events that affected these families whose relatives were killed created the conditions for the development of a more complex and severe type of trauma response. The circumstances of their relatives' death, the treatment of family members by the military and police, the flawed Widgery investigation, and the persistent civil unrest and violence in Northern Ireland, constituted, we argue, a Type 2 trauma. Many family members display features of a complex PTSD reaction that may explain the persistence of their symptoms.

PTSD and the Troubles in Northern Ireland

There has been substantial research into the psychological impact of the Troubles in Northern Ireland and some attempts to apply PTSD concepts to the conflict. Several themes have emerged from these studies related to the use of coping mechanisms such as denial and distancing, habituation; resiliency and powerlessness, and social support (Cairns and Wilson, 1984, 1989). Recognition of delayed onset of trauma, chronicity of symptoms, and violence as a precursor to PTSD, regardless of personal or social variables, were important findings that may help us understand the over 30-year-old trauma suffered by the Bloody Sunday families (Curran et al., 1990; Kee et al., 1987; Loughrey et al., 1988; Joseph et al., 1994; Scott, Brooks and McKinley, 1995). Cairns and Wilson (1984, 1989) found that people who coped by using denial were less stressed by living in areas of high levels of perceived threat of, or actual, political violence; thus denial may be a protective factor in the face of violence. Those who appeared to be coping well in certain areas of Northern Ireland used denial and psychological distancing as their main defences to maintain stability in a threatening environment. Inability to achieve concrete change to the political and social condition in Northern Ireland led to distancing as an adaptive response. Most people in Northern Ireland appear to have managed to cope with the stress from the Troubles except for a small minority who were at risk of traumatisation because they had a realistic understanding of their situation and could not use denial or distancing to alleviate their stress.

Kee et al. (1987) surveyed a litigant population (n=719) that sought redress following assassination attempts, sexual assaults, violent political assault such as kneecapping, and being taken hostage by terrorists. They also included victims of violent threats, casual witnesses with significant risk of injury, as in a bombing, and casual witnesses of a violent event (the largest group) who had no immediate threat of bodily harm. The majority of the sample was diagnosed with anxiety and depressive disorders. It was thought that 90 per cent of the study participants were 'malingerers' with no psychiatric illness and 23 per cent met the criteria for PTSD. The researchers found no significant association between the development of PTSD and factors such as unemployment, social class, religion, number of children, family history of psychiatric illness, early loss of parent or parent separation. Past psychiatric history, quality of marital relationship, previous alcohol intake, previous work record, life events before the incident, past criminal record, intelligence level and past medical history also could not be associated with the development of PTSD. There was no correlation between the seriousness of the threatening incident and the severity of the psychological reaction. Treatment included tranquillisers for 51 per cent, hypnotics for 35 per cent and antidepressants for 13 per cent of patients. There was a gradual reduction in use of medication, but a small group continued to take drugs for a year or more. Most were attended by their own physician, 11 per cent by psychiatric professionals, and 4.5 per cent required inpatient psychiatric care. Many people had returned to work before their case was settled. Kee et al. were concerned about the relationship of membership in a litigant population and the chronicity of symptoms, so they suggested further investigation.

Several researchers thereafter studied litigant populations. Loughrey et al. (1988) sought to determine the presence of PTSD in 499 victims of terrorist and civil violence in Northern Ireland in order to determine the validity of the diagnosis of PTSD. Symptoms commonly reported included hyper-arousal, such as startle reactions and sleep disturbance, intrusions and, to a lesser extent, nightmares. Intensification of symptoms through exposure to symbolic reminders of the event was found to be the most persistent symptom. Scott, Brooks and McKinley (1995), in a later study of yet another litigant population consisting of those affected by the bombing of PanAm flight 103 in Lockerbie (Scotland), confirmed the chronicity of symptoms in this group after 36 months.

Curran et al. (1990) studied the consequences of the Enniskillen bombing of 1987. Victims tended to minimise their symptoms but demonstrated high degrees of symptomatology, had severe symptoms of posttraumatic stress, and coped by distancing themselves psychologically from the intense feelings associated with the trauma. Many people were still symptomatic a year later, with those suffering severe injuries particularly prone to PTSD. Physical injury and recovery needs overshadowed the emotional trauma. There was a significant difference in the number of persons displaying symptoms of PTSD in their studies of the same population, first conducted in 1988 and then, in 1990. In 1988, 23 per cent of victims of terrorist violence were identified as suffering from PTSD, but in the 1990 study, 50 per cent demonstrated symptomatology. The researchers concluded that the result was due to very early assessment of the 1988 group, thus they could support the notion of delayed onset of PTSD. Persistent traumatic consequences were evident even eight years after the bombing. Residents of Enniskillen and a neighbouring town were asked to rate what they thought were the most salient events or changes over the past 50 years in Northern Ireland. Those who mentioned the bombing had significantly worse mental health outcomes than those who did not mention the event (Cairns and Lewis, 1999).

The Omagh bombing in 1998 which resulted in the deaths of 29 people and two unborn children in a busy shopping area was a particularly traumatic event not only for that community and the families of those killed, but also for health service workers. Luce et al. (2002) found, that despite the considerably increased availability of professional services in recent years, health service workers, especially nurses, were among the most traumatised, but many did not seek professional help for dealing with PTSD symptomatology. The authors concluded that more work needs to be done in agencies' disaster planning to meet the needs of groups that are most likely to witness horrific scenes, whether the event itself or in caring for victims. In the traumatic aftermath of the bombing McGarvey and Collins (2001) explored a number of perspectives to try to understand PTSD and develop interventions for those affected. They concluded that cognitive therapies show promise as effective modalities. Gillespie et al. (2002) concurred with this assessment and reported that cognitive behaviour therapies were most helpful in their study of 91 patients suffering PTSD as a consequence of the bombing. All 91 patients experienced substantial improvement in PTSD symptomatology after an average of eight sessions.

Preliminary research for the present work (Smyth and Hayes, 1994) suggested the presence of posttraumatic stress symptomatology and accompanying health consequences among the

Bloody Sunday family members (Hayes and Campbell, 1999). Shevlin and McGuigan (2003) also measured psychological distress among the family members and found a higher degree of PTSD symptomatology among immediate family members, and lesser distress among more distant relatives, such as first and second cousins. Among the immediate family members, PTSD was manifested with a higher degree of clinically significant reactions such as intrusions, avoidance and hyper-arousal 30 years after the event. Scores on the Impact of Life Event scales (Weiss and Marmar, 1997) for immediate family members paralleled those of comparison group members who had experienced natural disasters or combat situations elsewhere. The researchers concluded that the Bloody Sunday families may be suffering from cumulative stressors related to Bloody Sunday over the past 30 years. These had a negative impact on their psychological well being. It is also possible their symptoms were related to complicated bereavement or co-morbidity with depression. The potential for trans-generational transmission of trauma to the children of the immediate family is an area that requires further study. All of these studies in Northern Ireland have implications for the present work.

Grief, mourning and trauma

Bloody Sunday family members who participated in this work were children, adolescents or young adults at the time of the violent death of their parent or sibling, and they often spoke about their difficult grief process around those deaths. We present a theoretical discussion of grief, mourning and trauma as a background for understanding the complexities of trauma and the subsequent, complicated grieving experienced by the Bloody Sunday family members. The violent death of a sibling or parent which was perceived to have occurred in an unfair and unjust manner was psychologically damaging to family members and later events compounded the trauma by creating a culture of victim blaming. The usual funeral rituals and social services were largely unavailable to family members. The psychological needs of children were not addressed because of the magnitude of the trauma in the family and abnormal grieving by parents. This appears to have been compounded by the political climate, a lack of community and social service support, and media coverage which stigmatised the victims as criminals. The long-term consequences and impact of this trauma are still being felt as family members chronically process and try to deal with the trauma that has dominated their lives, often to the detriment of their health and family relationships. The family members' narratives presented in subsequent chapters, revealed their unmet psychological needs and also the implications that the Bloody Sunday trauma had for the victims' siblings and children as they parented their offspring born years after the event.

Grief and mourning

For most people, grief is the acute response to the experience of loss. It includes subjective feelings and particular behaviours, such as the painful loss of interest in life, dejection, irritability, numbness and apathy (Pynoos, 1985). One way of viewing the process of grief work is through observable behaviours. As time progresses, the grief behaviour gradually extinguishes from lack of reinforcement as the person takes on other behaviours not associated with the deceased (Dillenburger, 1994). Others have argued that thoughts and beliefs are just as important as behaviour in understanding how we grieve. Feelings, thoughts and behaviours associated with loss can be reignited at symbolic times such as anniversaries; however, this is short-lived and most people progress toward resolution. When grief is associated with violent death, however, the process is prolonged or impaired, as the narratives related by Bloody Sunday family members illustrate. Mourning is the lessening of grief over time as one adapts to a changed life situation (Horowitz, 1993). When the grief reaction is overwhelming or extremely persistent, interfering with work or relationships, it becomes pathological. Abnormal grief adds the elements of panic, self-hostility and self-blame. Unexpected, complicated death, experienced as unfair, along with social or economic difficulties such as loss of home or other relationships, increases the risk of a pathological response and the likelihood of depressive reactions. Support from others helps, and without it, mourning is difficult.

Children and grief

Many children under the age of 18 have experienced the death of a parent or sibling. Children are capable of grief and many of their responses to a loss are the same as adults, but there are important differences related to development, personality and culture (Pynoos, 1985). Young children have a short attention span and therefore are unable to spend long periods with grief work. Their sadness may go unnoticed as a result. They may be incapable of full participation in grief rituals such as funerals. Children seek to maintain attachment to the lost love object even though they understand intellectually that the person is dead. This and other defensive manoeuvres such as denying the significance of the loss help the child to cope. Adults, however, may see these behaviours as an indication that the child is not affected by the death. Children also are susceptible to the same maladaptive responses to grief and mourning as adults. In children, pathological grief may be manifested by severe behaviour problems and impaired social functioning. The death of a parent is always distressing for a child, however, when the death is violent, PTSD with all the accompanying symptoms, is often the result.

Children and trauma

Children and adolescents may experience PTSD after being involved in a disaster (Pynoos and Nader, 1993). Developmental issues influence how children respond to trauma, how they appraise threat, the meaning they attribute to the event, and how they recover and tolerate changes in their lives in the traumatic aftermath (Pynoos and Nader, 1993; Stallard and Law, 1994). The newborn infant of a traumatised mother can manifest symptoms of severe trauma such as hyperactivity, irritability and feeding problems, symptoms related to biochemical changes in the mother which were passed along to the unborn infant (Fredrick, 1985).

Children demonstrate symptomatology through play, drawings, re-enactments, traumatic dreams, avoidant or phobic behaviour, sleep disturbances, irritability, anger, separation anxiety, intrusions, conduct disturbances, hyper-alertness related to the event, enuresis and thumb sucking. They may not be interested in once pleasurable activities, may have memory disturbances and may lose acquired skills. Children may also experience dissociative reactions, particularly if they were in danger of compromised physical integrity. They may feel a sense of aloneness, fear that another trauma may occur, and may be pessimistic for their future prospects, including career, marriage and family (Pynoos and Nader, 1993). Consequences of PTSD in children attributable to neuro-physiological changes resulting from trauma include alterations in behaviour and self-concept that may affect the formation of the child's character. Adolescents may manifest PTSD through self-blaming, guilt or risk taking (Pynoos and Nader, 1993). If the traumatic event resulted in multiple traumas, as in a natural disaster which resulted in injury, death, separation from parents, or loss of home or community, they may be at increased risk of depression or anxiety disorder. As in the case of grieving children, parents, teachers and caregivers tend to minimise or fail to acknowledge the severity of pain that traumatised children or adolescents experience (Stallard and Law, 1994).

Grief and trauma

The relationship between grief and trauma is not well studied either in adults or children (Pynoos, 1985). Trauma and grief are different experiences but one event can trigger both responses. Trauma compromises the ego's capacity to deal with the work of grieving. If an individual is unable to work through the trauma, the grief process is aborted or delayed and may be triggered at a later time particularly if the trauma is not resolved. This may happen when the person reaches the same age as the deceased or during symbolic re-enactments like anniversaries. In the case of violent death, trauma may be prolonged by involvement with police and the justice system. The intrusive nature of trauma prevents the child from fantasising about the lost love object, an essential part of the child's grief work (Pynoos, 1985). Intrusions of horrific images block the important grief-work process of remembering, reminiscing and identifying with the lost parent. The child fears identification with the lost parent because he or she may fear violent death too. Funerals normally allow the child to see the parent intact and this can aid in the service of the identification process. In cases of violent death, the normal funeral and wake are not always possible.

Other trauma-related phenomena that interfere with grief work are survivor guilt, including revenge fantasies, and self-blame. In the presence of trauma, the child's ego is constricted, resulting in foreshortened life expectation, narrowing of life's choices and cognitive difficulties (Pynoos, 1985). Intrusions can interfere with schoolwork, and depression can retard cognitive and social development. The ego's priority is to deal with the trauma and this is accomplished at the expense of grieving and other activities. Psychic numbing, a symptom of PTSD which interferes with the grief process, can have long-term and serious consequences for the developing child.

Long-term consequences of trauma

The violent death of a parent can be stigmatising for a child, particularly if the death is recounted in the media. This stigmatisation might lead to the loss of social supports. Families often avoid references to the deceased, thus isolating the child further to deal with the symptoms of the trauma. Family reunions are avoided if they occur around the time of the death and if the gathering does occur, no mention is made of the deceased. Spontaneous mention of the deceased is ignored or unwelcome. Parents fear that discussing the trauma may cause additional damage and they often become upset when children talk about the trauma. Children learn to remain quiet to avoid upsetting their parents (Yule, 1994, a and b; Luce et al., 2002). Children need encouragement and permission from parents and others to talk about what happened and how and why it happened (Stallard and Law, 1994).

People exposed to prolonged danger may develop PTSD as a maladaptive response to the danger. Parents in such environments may develop inappropriate child-rearing practices that could impede the child's development. For example, behaviour of punitive parents, intended to safeguard the child, may teach him or her that aggressiveness and violence are appropriate methods for social control (Garbarino, Kostelny and DuBrow, 1991). A different approach to keeping children safe is for parents to provide an alternative to the negative culture of violence, particularly in politically charged and violent environments. If parents are not successful in this, their children may be at risk of recruitment into violent groups. Children's moral development may be arrested through the incorporation of a vendetta mentality. Parents and teachers should be role models and help the child move beyond this; however, they are often silenced by extreme elements in politically charged environments.

Living in harm's way, coupled with economic distress, political conflict, terrorism, and racism, is very stressful. In extreme circumstances, family life can appear normal but it is achieved at great psychological cost. These problems can affect a child's physical, emotional and moral development more than a specific traumatic event. Political and religious ideology may provide some support necessary to cope with trauma but these institutions may also retard the development of political solutions. Lack of ideology, however can promote despair, intra-group negativism and violence.

Cairns and Wilson (1984) and Blease (1983) noted that people in Northern Ireland who lived on the fringes of troubled areas tended to suffer more chronic and long-term anxiety. Those who lived in violent areas developed acute, less lasting effects. Children, however, responded to parental cues, particularly those of the mother (Blease, 1983).

Not all children exposed to trauma go on to develop PTSD. Mediating factors include supportive, available parents, and an uninterrupted daily routine. Factors that lead to positive coping include avoiding withdrawal, activity orientation, and at least one stable relationship with a parent or other adult (Garbarino, Kostelny and DuBrow, 1991). Providing this type of environment may be complicated if parents are also traumatised as in wartime or after a natural disaster. When parents are coping reasonably well in such difficult environments, the child will survive intact, however, if parents are pushed beyond their capacity, the child will deteriorate and possibly die from lack of care and protection (Garbarino, Kostelny and DuBrow, 1991).

Strategies of intervention for children who have experienced a trauma must address multiple issues because in a disaster, children experience multiple losses and have to work through all of them. They require protection from further adversity and treatment of the many disorders that could arise (Pynoos and Nader, 1993). Children need truth, and reassurance that someone will love them and care for them. If a disaster occurred at night, children try to avoid bedtime, so they will need help in talking about their fears. Schools can be instrumental in helping children to adapt to trauma. Artwork and drawings are helpful strategies (Gibson, 1996). The school also plays a role in crisis management, since child traumas do occur in schools or involve schoolmates. Children must process reactions, receive help in understanding their responses, and have the opportunity to talk about death and dying. Helping professionals can determine those most at risk and who need long-term therapy (Pynoos and Nader, 1993).

Helping people with PTSD

Victims of traumatic events often need immediate practical help, a safe environment, and later anticipatory guidance about the coping process, predicting symptoms, reality testing, and the need to reconstruct the event over and over, to tell the story and confront the experience (Brom and Kleber, 1989; Hunt, 1997; van der Kolk and Fisler, 1995). In the immediate post-crisis period there is usually chaos and lack of information, so in some circumstances it can be helpful for trained personnel to talk to survivors and their relatives to organise the rescue, and to see that victims or bodies are handled with dignity. People are shocked and numb, but need basic information and details about what happened and who has been killed or injured. Families often need helpers to be with them as they identify bodies, visit the site of the disaster, place flowers and make funeral arrangements. People will begin to face their loss of a loved one or their own injuries, or what their future will look like (Gibson, 1996). Some will experience posttraumatic stress reactions with intrusions, sleep disorders, anger at inability to change the situation, and guilt: 'If only I had done something different' is a common response. Those most affected may feel overwhelmed and alone as attention from media and friends decreases. Adaptation occurs when the person can acknowledge the past and integrate change with less pain. They must grieve the loss of loved ones and also the persons they used to be.

In the aftermath of natural and human-made disasters, as people try to understand why the disaster happened, angry responses are not unusual (Gibson, 1996). Anger at the time of a natural disaster is more generalised rather than focused anger that can be directed at an organisational system or a human-made horror. The media usually fuels speculation about whom to blame and influences people's responses, particularly a desire for retaliation. Many immediate family members of the victims, however, do not call for retaliation. Their pain is too great, and they do not wish to inflict this pain on others.

People need to know that help is available if they need it. A variety of approaches have been used to help people who suffer from symptoms of posttraumatic stress, ranging from clinical strategies to community-based interventions. Most traumatised people do not seek professional therapy, but helping professionals have learned over the recent past that the general aims of assistance after the trauma include crisis intervention, stimulating healthy ways of coping through adequate nutrition, exercise, early recognition of disorders, and psychotherapy if needed to help victims tell their story (Brom and Kleber, 1989). Processing the trauma and preventing more serious sequelae depend on avoidance of reliance on substances, education about the stress response, and judicious use of medication. People need reassurance that the reactions they are experiencing are normal, that there are ways to overcome their feelings of helplessness, and that there are resources in the community that can help (Ochberg, 1993).

Since there are known physiological alterations occurring in the brain of persons with PTSD, it seems reasonable that drugs which can diminish physiological activity would alleviate abnormal sleep patterns, hyper-arousal or anxiety (Friedman, 1993). Most psychotropic drugs, including antidepressant and anxiolytic agents, some anti-convulsants and lithium have been used in treatment of PTSD. While few controlled studies have examined the effects of psychotropic drugs in persons with PTSD, there is a growing sense that drugs, particularly certain selective serotonin reuptake inhibitors (SSRIs) help. Anti-psychotics, however, have no place in routine treatment of PTSD. Neurophysiological alterations may make PTSD patients more susceptible to addiction, so any agent that has addictive potential is not advisable with these people (Friedman, 1993).

Sedation with anti-anxiety medications, on a day-to-day basis only, and not in combination with other medications or alcohol, can be useful in the management of insomnia. Antidepressants should not be used in the immediate phase of loss. Patients in acute phases should be cautioned about driving or operating machinery or other situations requiring alertness, since they may have trouble concentrating or may experience startle reactions that could cause them to lose control. If symptoms persist more than a few weeks, brief psychotherapy is indicated. Therapy should continue for about twelve weeks in order to establish an alliance with a therapist who can help the person with reactions to the trauma, examine conflicts, developmental issues and coping styles that predispose towards vulnerability during the trauma and aftermath. A safe, communicative relationship allows the person a sense of relief and provides opportunities to examine the event, to confront the trauma, reorganise one's schemas and to work through loss rekindled by termination of the therapy.

The Bloody Sunday stories as recounted by family members illustrate for us the kinds of experiences that form the basis for the PTSD syndrome. Their responses in the aftermath of Bloody Sunday were typical of children or adolescents whose needs were overlooked by distraught parents who were emotionally, and often physically, unable to meet their needs. The traumatic deaths of parents and siblings, living in an environment of ongoing violence, and lack of social supports following the event, have, we believe, seriously impacted family members' capacity to grieve normally and to resolve trauma, and have profoundly affected their health and well being thereafter.

Storytelling and trauma resolution

Horowitz (1976) provides us with an elegant conceptualisation of the sequelae of trauma and internal processes that help or hinder the integration and resolution of PTSD. He hypothesised that people form internal cognitive/emotional schemas, re-presentations of past perceptions about the world and self that include 'conclusions' about them. A basic schema might be a sense that the world is a good and safe place or that people are basically good, and that bad things only happen to bad people. Another might involve one's personal and bodily integrity including boundaries essential to the sense of self. A trauma shatters existing schemas, especially when the experience departs markedly from how one views the world. Serious deviations result in a more severe response. Storytelling can be an important mechanism that can help in closure, with narratives particularly important in the 'working through' phase of coping with a trauma (Horowitz, 1976). Trauma victims use language to externalise the trauma as they experienced it and re-experience it. Language helps people achieve catharsis, become empowered and able to speak for themselves, relieve their pressures, and gain increased self-control and self-esteem (Herbst, 1992). Failure to work through may lead to chronic problems, even illness (Horowitz, 1976, 1993; Janet, 1920; van der Kolk, 1994).

Linguistic retrieval of traumatic memories allows the experience to be integrated into a person's life experiences. Storytelling, no matter how halting at first, is essential to recovery from trauma (Brom and Kleber, 1989). Not every one can completely recover from horrific events, particularly people rendered paralysed by inaction at the time of the trauma (van der Kolk, 1994). By telling the story, however, the 'person can look back at what happened; he has given it a place in his life story, his autobiography, and thereby in the whole of his personality' (van der Kolk and van der Hart, 1991: 448). Telling the story and integrating the trauma into one's life is necessary for healing to occur and for formulating positive schemas that allow one to live in his or her now-changed world. Storytelling has been a technique used for both public and private disclosures among Holocaust survivors, victims in civil wars and among victims of sexual abuse (Harvey et al., 1991; Aron, 1992; Herbst, 1992). Telling one's personal story about a horrific event cannot change what happened, but as a form of socio-therapy, it can help to heal and places blame appropriately, away from the victim, to the perpetrators (Aron, 1992). This process has only recently begun for Bloody Sunday family members.

Summary

In this chapter, we have reviewed a range of perspectives on the concept of PTSD and its long-term consequences, and aspects of the interaction of trauma, grief and mourning for children, adolescents and adults. We examined PTSD within a historical context and in terms of relevant biophysical, psychological and psychosocial theories that have contributed to understanding symptomatology, prevention of serious sequelae, management and resolution of trauma. We viewed narrative as central to healing. Such theories are helpful for us in making sense of some of the narrative detail which emerged from interviews with Bloody Sunday family members who chronically process the traumatic loss of their loved one at the hands of the state. It is important, in this respect, to examine how family members have coped with their reaction to this traumatic event in Northern Ireland and in the often violent years which followed.

4 The study methodology

We have been keenly interested in finding ways to explore the psychological and social impact of Bloody Sunday on family members whose relative had been killed that day. Although there have been quantitative studies of the Troubles and their impact on various populations in Northern Ireland (Cairns and Darby, 1998; Cairns and Wilson, 1984, 1989; Curran et al., 1990; Kee et al., 1987; Loughrey et al., 1988) by the time of the 25th anniversary of Bloody Sunday in 1997, there had been few attempts to apply qualitative approaches for this purpose. Researchers in Northern Ireland and elsewhere (Cairns and Dawes, 1996; McWhirter, 1983; Nagata, 1990; Solkoff, 1981, 1992; Whyte, 1983) however, called for qualitative approaches in order to understand the impact of traumatic experiences. We have assumed that family members suffered from PTSD as defined by the *DSM-IV* (American Psychiatric Association, 1994), so we utilised a primarily qualitative approach with interviews complemented by two brief measures of psychological health to explore and describe narrative content and form around the significance of the Bloody Sunday trauma for the family members at the time of the 25th anniversary (Hayes, 2000). Many of the same family members participated in further interviews five years later.

Rationale for the qualitative approach

A number of researchers in Northern Ireland, who were optimistic initially about the general mental health and coping of populations during the Troubles, eventually expressed concern that research questions asked and study samples recruited may not have been the most appropriate for assessing the impact of community violence. They were also aware of the fact that, until relatively recently, the impact of a single trauma within the context of ongoing trauma, had not been investigated to any great extent. No one really knew what the long-term effects of continuous political violence might be, particularly for young people who seemed to be resilient despite the Troubles (Toner, 1990; Cairns and Dawes, 1996). In response to these perceived limitations in the literature, we used a qualitative methodology with narrative inquiry or storytelling research technique, to explore the long-term impact of the trauma which affected the Bloody Sunday family members.

Although it can be argued that the events of Bloody Sunday alone might have led to a Type 1 trauma response for many family members, the aftermath of the event, the victim blaming, the damaging effects of the Widgery Tribunal, and years of armed strife in Derry and elsewhere in Northern Ireland, may have compounded the trauma and qualified it as a Type 2 trauma (Terr, 1990). We sought to examine this proposition by allowing family members to tell their story, not only as a vehicle for understanding the impact of trauma but also by providing them an opportunity for healing (van der Kolk, 1994). The findings report the views and perceptions of the family members who participated in the study and are not meant to provide generalisable data about the population of all Bloody Sunday family members in Derry.

Narrative inquiry is a useful way for exploring individual experiences in depth, and for understanding the impact of trauma. The storytelling technique includes attending to, telling about, transcribing, analysing and reading experience (Riessman, 1993). Attending to experience refers to the selection of a topic from an infinite selection, in this case, the story of Bloody Sunday. Telling about experience relates to the particular technique used for the telling, for example, the use of an open-ended interview schedule to elicit participating family members' experiences of Bloody Sunday. Transcribing experience captures the entire content of the narrative, which includes the story and the way in which it was told. Analysing the experience extracts its impact, derived from the storyteller's own words which are organised into recurring themes by the researcher. The reading of experience shapes the stories into a text for interpretation by the reader.

The study instruments

Family members were asked to tell their story of Bloody Sunday. Open-ended questions were designed to elicit the story of the event in the broadest fashion possible to enable respondents to choose the manner and extent of telling without excessive prompting from the researcher. For example, the following questions were used:

- Tell me the story of what happened on Bloody Sunday.
- What has changed over the years: content, details, frequency, length of the story, the way it is told?
- How has Bloody Sunday affected you?
- How have your attitudes toward Bloody Sunday changed over the years?

The questions were designed to determine the impact of the trauma for the participants, and to ascertain if the memories and attitudes related to the trauma were fixed or evolving. Traumatic memories tend to be fixed and unchanging (van der Kolk, 1994), but changing attitudes might be an indication of trauma integration as people attempt to include the trauma into their life perspective, as in forming new schemas (Horowitz, 1976). Two quantitative measures also were used to complement narrative data. These were the PTSD Symptom Inventory (Hayes and Campbell, 1999) and the GHQ-12 questionnaire (Goldberg and Hillier, 1979; Goldberg and Williams, 1988). The PTSD Symptom Inventory is a researcher-designed 12-item questionnaire in a Likert scale format which assesses the presence of PTSD symptoms as defined by the *DSM-IV* (American Psychiatric Association, 1994) as they related to the event of Bloody Sunday. The participant was requested to choose along a seven point continuum from 1, 'not at all' to 7, 'all the time'. The following are examples of such questions:

- Have you ever had a period of time when you kept having painful memories of Bloody Sunday even when you tried not to think about it?
- Have you ever had a period of time when you found yourself in a situation that reminded you of Bloody Sunday and then you acted and felt as though it was happening all over again?

This inventory was originally adapted from one designed by Hough and Vega (1990) in their work that assessed PTSD symptomatology in the aftermath of a massacre at a McDonald's restaurant in San Ysidro, California. The instrument was piloted in the

Derry community by Smyth and Hayes in 1994 and modified to make it more manageable for participants. It now consists of twelve items. This inventory is not designed to make a diagnosis of PTSD but it provides a measure of possible symptomatology which may be seen in conjunction with narrative data derived from the interviews with family members. The possible range of scores on this instrument is 12 to 84, with higher scores indicating increased potential for PTSD symptomatology. Prior use of the Hough and Vega (1990) questionnaire showed high face validity when compared with *DSM-III* diagnostic criteria. A panel of expert psychiatrists, social workers and psychologists, colleagues of Patrick Hayes, established content validity for the instrument used in the present study. Internal consistency reliability (alpha reliability) for the instrument was shown to be 0.90.

The second questionnaire, the General Health Questionnaire (GHQ) has been used in Northern Ireland in several community based studies (Cairns, 1988, 1989; Wilson and Cairns, 1987). There are several versions of the test, with 12, 28, 30 and 60 items each. The purpose of the test is to distinguish people with some form of psychological disturbance from those who are relatively healthy by detecting recent disruption of everyday life activities and the experience of subjective distress. The test does not claim that it is an aid in the differential diagnosis of various psychiatric disorders.

The GHQ scales have been used as brief, economical screening tools in clinical and research settings for rapid determination of psychiatric status. They are easily administered and may be helpful in detecting those persons who would benefit from a psychiatric referral. The scales have been tested over the past 25 years with reliabilities and tests of internal consistency and validity reported as high (Banks et al., 1980). The instrument used in this study, the GHQ-12, has been tested and shown to have a high degree of internal consistency, with Chronbach's alpha reported as high as 0.90 (Banks et al., 1980). The test is viewed as an adequate unidimensional measure of minor psychiatric disorder within and between populations (Banks et al., 1980). The GHQ-12 measures, in a four-point scale format, issues related to emotional health such as concentration, sleep disturbance, self-esteem, and levels of stress and depression. Respondents are instructed to underline one of four choices for each of the twelve items. For example, a selection of the first or second choice would depict no disturbance on that item and either of these choices would be scored as 0. A selection of either the third or fourth choice would indicate disturbance, and either of these choices would be scored as 1. Therefore, on the twelve-item scale, a minimum score is 0 and a maximum score is 12.

Questions on the instrument include a request for participants to consider any medical complaints and how their health in general has been in the recent past. For example, have you recently:

- Been able to concentrate on whatever you are doing?
- Lost much sleep over worry?
- Been feeling unhappy and depressed?
- Been feeling reasonably happy, all things considered?

Higher scores equate to higher levels of psychological disorder. Use of the GHQ in samples of subjects can be used to compute the average score of the sample, or the number and percentage that are cases. With the GHQ-12, a score over 2 is considered to be an indication of morbidity or 'caseness' (Banks et al., 1980). A score of 2 is considered the threshold for caseness. Although the GHQ was not designed to measure PTSD, it has been used in that way (Goldberg and Hillier, 1979) and does measure the extent of underlying disturbances or psychological distress. The GHQ-12 was used with Bloody Sunday respondents to measure their general mental health and state in the world, particularly in the recent past, which for participants was the period immediately surrounding the 25th anniversary of the event (Goldberg and Williams, 1988). The researcher chose this instrument because of its simplicity and effective use in the United Kingdom and to provide a culturally appropriate counter measure to the US researcher-designed PTSD Symptom Inventory.

The field process

Patrick Hayes was originally from the Bogside area of Derry, although he left many years before the start of the Troubles and has lived in the United States since. Over the course of several visits to Derry, he developed a trusting relationship with Bloody Sunday family members after meeting some of them at the Finucane Centre in Derry. During the meeting he presented the concept of PTSD and the parallels between the dynamics of childhood sexual abuse and family members' experience of Bloody Sunday. The audience resonated with this theme since some indeed had been abused in multiple ways at the hands of the peacekeeping forces. These family members, some of whom participated in the 1994 study (Smyth and Hayes), introduced Hayes to other Bloody Sunday family members who were willing to participate in an ongoing study.

The study sample

The sample of 26 family members was drawn from twelve of the 14 families whose relative was killed on Bloody Sunday. Participants were children, adolescents or young adults at the time of Bloody Sunday. Of these, 24 were siblings of a person killed, and two were children of a person killed. A total of ten of these family members attended the march on 30 January 1972. None witnessed the killing of their relative, but most of those present witnessed violence. Several saw dead bodies on the streets. One family with three respondents, in addition to losing a sibling, had a father seriously wounded. Approximately 50 per cent of the respondents were active members of the Bloody Sunday Justice Campaign, a group of family members and others interested in seeking redress around the perceived injustice of the events of Bloody Sunday and its aftermath. Involvement for most participants, however, was recent and related to the forthcoming 25th anniversary. Other family members who were not involved in the campaign were also invited to participate in the study. Demographic data for each participant included age, gender, marital status, number of children, educational level attained, occupational status, and a category describing the participant's relationship to the deceased. This data is presented in Table 1.

The family members completed the PTSD Symptom Inventory and the GHQ-12 and participated in in-depth, audiotaped interviews of 30 to 45 minutes at their homes or at the home of a relative in or near Derry. Three interviews could be described as

Table 1 Characteristics of participants (n=26)

	Frequency		Frequency
Age		**Number of**	
30–34	3	**children**	
35–39	3	0	1
40–44	6	1–3	14
45–49	7	4–6	9
50–54	6	7–8	2
55–59	1		
		Years of education	
Gender		8–10	10
Male	12	11–12	9
Female	14	12+	3
		Missing	4
Employment			
Employed	13	**Relationship to**	
Unemployed	13	**victim**	
		Sibling	24
Marital status		Child	2
Married	21		
Other	5		

'family interviews' with several members of a family participating in a manner which they preferred. In two families the interaction proved to be highly emotive and seemed to provide a catharsis. Both families acknowledged that the experience was healing.

Additional fieldwork conducted close to the 30th anniversary of Bloody Sunday involved a similar interview process and included eleven participants, all siblings of the men killed on Bloody Sunday. Ten of these family members had also participated in the 25th anniversary interviews.

Data analysis: quantitative data

The Statistical Package for the Social Sciences (SPSS) was used to calculate the total scores, means and ranges for both the PTSD Symptom Inventory and the GHQ-12. The mean PTSD Symptom Inventory score was 48 with a range from 18 to 83. The maximum possible score was 84. For the ten respondents who attended the march on 30 January 1972, the mean PTSD Symptom Inventory score was 53. The mean score for the age group 40–50 was 51, three points higher than the mean of the overall sample, and 19 points higher than for the group under age 40. PTSD Symptom Inventory sub-scales, composed of questions grouped into clusters which depict distinct areas of symptomatology from the *DSM-IV*, included intrusions, numbing, hyper-arousal, hyper-vigilance and survivor guilt. Intrusions, hyper-arousal and numbing accounted for higher mean scores in those clusters.

Studies among ageing veterans suggest that as people age, structural and cognitive changes in the brain, brain changes related to PTSD, and the breakdown of previously successful coping strategies such as avoidance, may account for increased symptomatology, particularly the return of intrusions (Hunt, 1997). This may be the case for those Bloody Sunday family members over age 40 who represented two-thirds of the study participants.

The mean GHQ-12 score was 4.9, with a range of 12, high score of 12 and low of 0. The mean score for those who attended the march was 4.4. Of the ten family members who attended the march, six met the criteria for 'threshold caseness' or 'caseness',

Table 2 PTSD symptom inventory and GHQ-12 mean scores and ranges

PTSD symptom inventory	M	R	GHQ-12	M	R
Intrusions	15.8	24.0	Concentration	0.80	2.0
Numbing	10.8	18.0	Lost sleep	0.85	2.0
Hyper-arousal	13.1	18.0	Feeling useful	0.39	2.0
Hyper-vigilance	4.4	6.0	Make decisions	0.39	2.0
Survivor guilt	2.6	6.0	Constant strain	0.89	2.0
			Overcome difficulties	0.50	2.0
Overall PTSD score	48.0	65.0	Enjoy normal activity	0.65	2.0
			Face up to problems	0.46	2.0
			Unhappy/depressed	0.73	2.0
			Lose self-confidence	0.69	2.0
			Feeling worthless	0.37	2.0
			Feel happy	0.39	2.0
			Overall GHQ-12 score	4.90	12.0

a score ≥ 2 as determined by the GHQ-12 scoring guidelines. Table 2 summarises means, ranges, PTSD Symptom Inventory overall and sub-scale scores, and GHQ-12 overall and individual item scores. Based on the data derived from these two measures as completed by a sample of family members, we concluded that participants demonstrated significant PTSD symptomatology and general psychological disturbance related to Bloody Sunday. Notably, Shevlin and McGuigan (2003) used the Impact of Events scale-revised (Weiss and Marmar, 1997) and also found considerable PTSD symptomatology among a larger sample of Bloody Sunday family members around the time of the 30th anniversary. Symptomatology extended beyond the siblings of the men killed to their children, nieces, nephews and cousins, thus suggesting transgenerational consequences for this trauma. All of these findings lay the groundwork for understanding the impact of the event of Bloody Sunday on the family members who shared their stories at the time of the 25th anniversary and then, five years later.

Data analysis: qualitative data

Patton's strategy for analysing qualitative data generated from interviews (1990: 377) was useful to us in analysing the transcriptions derived from interviews with the Bloody Sunday family members. As with Riessman (1993), Patton's suggestions include telling the entire story and relating critical incidents, as well as describing places and locations, presenting people or groups, describing important processes such as control, recruitment, decision-making, socialisation and communication, and illuminating issues. The data generated from interviewing such numbers of people is substantial and requires organisation in the process of analysis. Content analysis used in the present study to organise the data, 'is the process of identifying, coding and categorising the primary patterns in the data ... analysing the content of interviews and observations' (Patton, 1990: 381). This type of classification of qualitative data allows the researcher to seek similar patterns and themes from the bulk of the narrative data. We utilised NUD*IST (Non-Numerical Unstructured Data Indexing, Searching and Theorising) software to analyse the interview transcriptions for similarities, recurrent themes and reports of experiences.

The transcripts were first imported into NUD*IST as text files. Nodes, a term NUD*IST uses to define containers for information, were created and named, using respondents' words whenever possible. Each node was assigned a numerical 'address' and may have several 'children' with an address of their own. In a manner similar to Patton's classification system, segments of narrative were distributed or coded into the appropriate node according to themes identified from the narrative data. For example, the node in this work coded as 'Hearing the News' at address 15 has one 'child' named 'Immediate Reaction' at address 151. 'Immediate Reaction' has five 'children', with distinct addresses. The 'children' are: 'Crying' at address 1511; 'Disbelief', 1512; 'Anger', 1513; 'Revenge' 1514; and 'Blank Memories' at address 1515. All nodes and their 'children' contain segments of narrative, researcher field notes and theoretical literature related to the theme, for example, (Horowitz, 1997), the initial response to a trauma. Figure 1 depicts the themes which emerged from portions of the data and presents in diagrammatic form several segments of a NUD*IST informational 'Index Tree' with nodes and 'children'. The root of the tree is the compiled narrative about Bloody Sunday at address 1. Themes derived from the narratives and interpreted within the context of the PTSD conceptual framework (Herman, 1992; Horowitz, 1993; Gibson, 1996; van der Kolk, 1994) illustrate the impact and significance of the Bloody Sunday trauma on family members from the day of the traumatic event onward. Patrick Hayes in subsequent meetings with family members validated his interpretations of these themes and their significance.

Study limitations

This was a non-random sample of Bloody Sunday family members, but every effort was made to represent all families of those killed, participants on the march as well as non-participants. Attempts were made to locate family members who were not participants in the Bloody Sunday Justice Campaign. Of the two families not represented, one had no surviving siblings or children and the other family was not available for participation. This study sample was small and none of the quantitative data from the study is generalisable to any group. However, it provided a

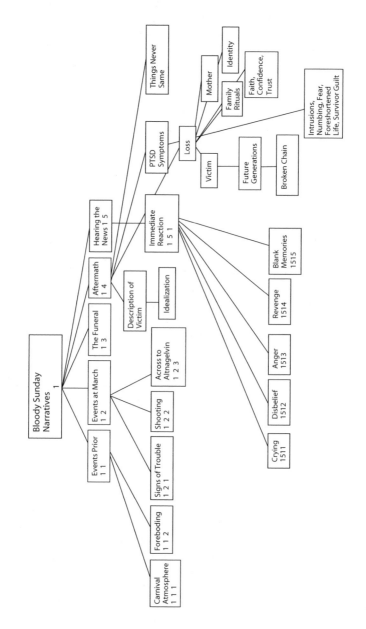

Figure 1 Segment of a NUD*IST Index Tree used to organise narratives

description of the sample and a means to corroborate interview data. The qualitative methodology provided the opportunity to relate the story of Bloody Sunday as the participating family members experienced it, in rich narratives which described the impact of that day on their lives. Patrick Hayes also periodically checked with participants to assure the trustworthiness of the reported narratives and to assure against bias in his interpretation.

Summary

In this chapter, we presented the study methodology, sample selection, procedures, data analysis, findings from the PTSD Symptom Inventory and the GHQ-12 along with the rationale for a qualitative approach complemented by quantitative measures. The qualitative analysis has helped to identify themes useful for illuminating the experiences of Bloody Sunday family members. These themes are elaborated upon in subsequent chapters with enough of the participants' own words to allow the reader to evaluate the researcher's inferences. Links to theoretical literature discussed in previous chapters provide a framework for interpreting data and themes that emerged from interviews.

5 Bloody Sunday, 30 January 1972

A number of writers have pieced together the events of Bloody Sunday (McClean, 1997; McCann, Shiels and Hannigan, 1992; Mullan, 1997; Pringle and Jacobson, 2000; Walsh, 2000). The narratives we present here and in later chapters complement these earlier works. They detail what happened prior to the trauma, the immediate reaction to the violence, the funeral, and the traumatic aftermath. Family members of those killed provided dramatic examples of the capacity of a tragedy such as this to make indelible marks on the psyche (Janet, 1920; van der Kolk, 1994).

Bloody Sunday has become well publicised recently in television documentaries and motion pictures. However, the words of the Bloody Sunday family members convey their unique perspective about what happened that day and in its aftermath. They told their stories as they smoked cigarettes, and shared tea and biscuits in their kitchens or the front room. They wept, laughed, wrung their hands or gestured emphatically to underscore a point. Some were frantic in their pain. Others were flat in their speech, sat quietly or were very soft spoken. They sat in chairs or on the floor, sometimes in groups, sometimes with their children or other family members present, but usually alone. Their narratives provide an opportunity for the readers of this book to expand their knowledge about PTSD and to gain insights into the consequences of the trauma that occurred on 30 January 1972. Family members' intrusions, denial, a sense of foreshortened life, survivor guilt, and their long-delayed process of 'working through' trauma help the reader to understand the experience of trauma and its sequelae.

The beginning of the day

Usually, the family members' stories began with the assembly of the marchers. As participants or onlookers, they felt 'easy go lucky' and 'jovial' that afternoon. This was 'the greatest thing that ever happened' for so many of them. People were happy and there was 'a carnival atmosphere because of the size of the crowd, about 25,000'. Their eyes were alive with excitement as they recalled the bishop blessing the marchers. The march proceeded down the hill from Creggan towards William Street. Family members recalled minute details very clearly. One man remembered standing near Aloysius School where the march began on that bright, crisp January day, digging his heel into the ground and 'feeling the hardness of it'. Others remembered singing the civil rights song of the time 'We shall overcome'. A family member who was eight years old at the time of the march, begged to be allowed to participate, but he was left at home. He described watching his brother go to the march without him. His last memory of his brother replays like a filmstrip frame by frame, details about ordinary things, re-told in a repetitive, hypnotic manner:

> He was coming out, putting on his coat in the living room and telling my mother that he was going down to the march, and I asked to go along to it, so I did. My mother wouldn't let me, or he didn't want to take me, I think. I cried after him that day and I had to bend up over the window to look out. I watched him the whole way until he disappeared over behind houses. He had a camera over his shoulder. I always have that memory of him of walking across the street, fading away.
>
> I watched him because I wanted to go with him that day. I watched him walk over. I've that memory always in my mind, for I looked out the window and I watched him just walk over, over the street and he walked over.

In spite of all the excitement of participating in the march, many family members recalled feeling very uneasy given the politically charged climate in Derry at that time. Some parents forbade their children to go to the march. Parental concerns, however, were dismissed by thoughts of experiencing 'a bit of the craic [fun]' and going to hear Bernadette Devlin, a local politician and activist, 'making a mouth of herself'. Most of the girls stayed home, but boys 'being 16 and 17 years of age, of course went'.

Many family members experienced premonitions of trouble prior to the march and continue to feel guilty that they were not more proactive in possibly preventing their brothers' deaths. One family member had surveyed the march route the day before, took photographs and noted military activity in the area and 'should have known' there was going to be trouble. Another 'had a gut feeling all day there was something not quite right'. One family member remembered telling his wife, 'There is going to be murder here today ... There was going to be an awful lot of heads busted.' He did not, however, anticipate killing. Yet another recalled feelings of dread the night before the march: 'Something's going to happen the 'morrow. If there's shooting, I was going to get it.' He had reservations about his younger brother's participation in the march and 'didn't actually like the sound of it ... had bad feelings about it ... don't know what it was.' He was not injured, but his brother was one of the 13 killed. The older sister of a young man killed felt she should have heeded what she believed in retrospect 'must have been a warning' the night before the march. Someone had shot a bullet through the bathroom window.

Family members consistently reported the beginning of trouble with precise attention to detail. There was 'a longish helicopter and it was flying pretty low over us at the corner of William Street and Albert Street and one of them [a soldier] was hanging out of the door of the helicopter giving the crowd the finger'. At the top of William Street was the first time they saw that there were 'soldiers on the ground. There was quite a lot of them and they were well armed.' A family member recalled the beginning of unrest at barrier 14, sometimes described as 'Aggro Corner':

> As the carnival passed, you could see paratroopers' red berets. We never knew what a paratrooper was or what would stand a paratrooper out from an ordinary soldier, but these red berets were clear to be seen. So we hurled abuse at them, and then they started the [dye] cannon. People got antagonised because there was very little [space] to go in William Street and the march couldn't go no further. Tempers started to rise.

The marchers were diverted to the Free Derry Corner (the entrance to the Bogside which was not in British control). They approached an army barricade on William Street, a common place for young people to riot against the army and police in the previous months. A family member, a young marcher that day, went to within a few feet of the barricade with 'soldiers on the other side and shouting and carrying on was going on'. Once the dye cannons were used, he was actually more concerned about anticipating his father's wrath at a ruined coat. This was more upsetting to him than what had now turned into what he thought was a 'normal' riot and he left, unaware of what had happened to his fellow marchers until much later.

Suddenly, on William Street, there were 'sharp cracks'. Panicked marchers made it clear that there was 'big trouble'. They had not heard rifle shots before, only plastic bullet shots. Realising the seriousness of the situation, a family member whose younger brother was somewhere in the crowd tried to dismiss his growing fear, 'He's [his brother] the sensible one in our family. He wouldn't take part in no rioting, no violence. Better go find him.'

A family member who was an adolescent at the time ran away from the crowd and the soldiers and nearly fell into a small walled garden in Glenfadda Park, a housing estate. A woman fell in front of him. He lifted her over the wall and at that point he heard multiple shots, rubber bullets he supposed at first, but he suddenly realised that it was live ammunition. He was incredulous as he saw 'Stones came out of the wall about 20 foot up. Now that alarmed me! I knew it was live ammunition but it was high and I thought, "Well, they are just putting the pressure on and they are just scaring us."'

So he waited for a time in Glenfadda, how long he is not sure, facing towards the Rossville barricade. There was gas everywhere, shouting and screaming. He was feeling very isolated when suddenly three soldiers with gas masks and rifles appeared out of the gas clouds. He then saw 'thousands of people laying flat on the road.' One of them shouted to him, 'Don't come out, they are shooting from the walls!'

Another family member witnessed one of the fatal shootings. He had recalled this only recently, a memory perhaps triggered by the publicity surrounding the 25th anniversary. As the victim of the shooting fell to the ground, he heard someone in the crowd shout, 'Hit the deck, they are firing from the walls!' At that point, he remembered, 'I did exactly that, because I knew there was firing from the walls. I got on my stomach and got as far as Joseph Place. I didn't know how many people had been shot until the next day.'

In an otherwise logical and detailed account, he could not recall details of experiences that spanned a ten-minute period, from the scene of the shooting until he arrived home. This memory gap, which may indicate repressed memories (American Psychiatric Association, 1994) at the time of the trauma, continued to trouble him:

> There is obviously more that happened that day, whilst I was on the march and after the march. What happened when I was getting from the Bogside Inn up to Creggan? I can't mind [remember] anything. I must have been talking to people. The only thing I can remember is the Bogside Inn and then the end of Dunree Gardens. In between I can't remember nothing.

The casualties began to mount as the shots continued. A family member remembered his attempts to aid one of the wounded. He learned later that his own brother was among those shot at the very moment he was assisting someone else. 'People were running and stampeding, shouting, "There's bad trouble over here. Couple shot." A guy says, "Shot. Plastic bullets and all?" "Real, serious shot." I says "Our [brother's name] is over there somewhere."' He continued:

> There was a boy shot in the chest. Somebody looked out the window and yelled, 'There's a body lying over there', but I ran from where I was across the road and I didn't see him [his brother]. I heard a crack behind me. All I was interested in was this body lying in the door. I got to the body and dragged him across the road to the house.

If he had just looked the other way, he would have found his brother. It never occurred to him that his brother 'would be lying a couple of yards' from where he was.

Outcry and denial

Horowitz (1993) describes the outcry and denial phases that characterise the immediate response to trauma. The outcry phase is a normal response to distressing news characterised by alarm, fear, and expressions as 'Oh, no!' or 'Oh my God!' or a scream or sob. The denial phase is reflected in exclamations like 'This can't be true!' or incomprehension, manifested by a stunned stare. Some people mount temporary defences to cope with the emergency, but they will experience the outcry phase in some manner, externally or internally at a later time. Outcry is manifested then as panic, enraged destructiveness, giving up, or being overwhelmed by emotional responses which may totally impair the adaptive process. Aspects of all of these responses to trauma are apparent in the words of the Bloody Sunday family members at the time they learned of their relative's death and in the days that followed.

Hearing the news: 'He's dead'

Hearing the news of the violent death of a loved one is extremely traumatising (Green, 1993). All family members had individualised stories about hearing of the death of their relative. Some Bloody Sunday family members kept 'getting up their hopes', but for most, complete chaos ensued when they heard the news. The sister of one of the young men killed remembered being at her boyfriend's house when one of his acquaintances knocked at the door and 'sort of came into the sitting room and was just sort of facing the front and he just sort of looked at me and said, "Your brother's been shot dead and your father's been shot too, but he is OK".' She walked around in circles not believing the news, acting 'like a robot' and crying, 'I have to go home, I have to go home.'

Members of one family heard rumours that one of the older sons had been injured. They were relieved when he arrived home safely, but their relief was short-lived. He was the one to break the news to the family that the rumour was true, but it was the youngest son who had been shot, not him. He recalled: 'I walked into the house and I had to say to my Mammy, my Ma was sitting on the sofa, "Jesus, Ma, [name] is dead." She thought he was shot in the leg. I said, "No, he's dead." The whole house went into an uproar.'

Another young man found the house filled when he returned home from the march, and his mother was crying. He remembered, 'My father called to me and he said "[name]'s dead". I just turned and walked out to the hall and I started crying, and got down on my

[75]

knees and just started crying.' In another family, when the sister of one of the young men killed arrived at her mother's house, everyone was standing outside, just talking, not thinking that any members of their family were involved. A neighbour and a priest walked up to them:

> One of the neighbours says '[brother's name] is dead now.' I remember going into the house then and I remember my mum was very sick, but she had nothing to throw up. I remember [sister's name] and me out in the toilet with her on her knees at the toilet bowl. I remember [sister's name] holding her head and her trying to be sick.

Bloody Sunday family members reported that family physicians prescribed large doses of Valium to mothers of some of the young men killed. Several family members reported that their mothers were sedated so heavily in the immediate aftermath of Bloody Sunday that they could not comprehend the death of their sons for weeks, or even years afterwards. Mothers were 'stupefied', given enough, a family member recalled, to 'put any normal person out for a week'. Some mothers had no memories of their sons in the coffin. However, one man spoke about his mother's response when she saw her youngest son in his coffin. He exclaimed loudly 'Jesus!' as he told how his mother lifted her dead son 'right out of the coffin, bodily lifted him up. She caught us unawares. So we had to dive and we had to put him back in again.' His father, he added sombrely, 'lost it in the bottle, y'know, in drink'.

A member of another family could not take in the news of the shootings, 'this bad dream', until he saw the picture of his dead brother on the front page of the newspaper the following morning. Another family member's brother confronted him in an agitated state, gave him the news of the death, but he remembers totally disregarding it as each shouted to the other:

> 'Jesus! What is wrong? Has he been arrested?' Because there was more fear of your father than you would have of the army arresting you, you know. 'Naw he's dead.' 'Naw, that's wrong.' Now he had definitely said to me that he was dead.

One woman remembered chiding her much younger brother for joking that their brother who was at the march had been shot, before anyone in the household knew about the deaths. It was an hour later when she heard the news. She had fallen asleep after dinnertime, and awoke when her father-in-law shook the chair. He said to her in a rather understated way, 'There is a bit of trouble down the town and I think one of your wee brothers has been hurt.' She went to her father's house and learned that, indeed her brother had been shot dead.

Children were very much aware of the bad news coming from the town. One family member, a 13-year-old girl at the time, was aware that there was trouble in the town and that people were killed. When she saw her older sister come to the house, she knew something was wrong, but thought the news was going to be about her mother who had been seriously ill in the weeks prior to Bloody Sunday:

> All week doctors were concerned about my mother because it was a major heart attack and she was recovering slowly. I didn't answer the door. My aunt went out and answered it and she came and said 'I have bad news for you.' I said, 'My mother's dead, isn't she?' She said, 'No, your brother's dead and your father's also injured.'

She confided she felt relieved that it was not her hospitalised mother who had died, but was really confused about the death of her brother, what had happened and why, and perhaps felt guilty at her relief that the news was about her brother, not her mother.

Young children especially had vivid memories of how they knew about the violent deaths of a sibling and a parent, but children's needs are often overlooked or ignored in the aftermath of a trauma, and this was the case for some of the youngsters whose sibling was killed (Pynoos and Nader, 1993; Stallard and Law, 1994). One man, an eight-year-old when the event occurred, remembered his father returning from the hospital:

> I mind [remember] everybody going into the house from all round the street. He come back and I watched him coming. It's as clear as if it happened an hour ago. I mind

him walking past the window with his head down and I knew. I was only eight years old at the time. I mind looking at him saying to myself, 'God, he doesn't look very happy anyway. There must be something wrong.' Well, he come in. He just said, 'Aye, it's [brother's name]. [brother's name] is dead', like that. Everything went haywire.

Another family member returned from the march and found his house filled with upset people who had heard of the shootings. His brother was missing. While his father went to the town to look for the missing son, he hoped and prayed that his brother was safe, but alternating between hope and despair, he 'got the feeling that he wasn't all right and it hurt'. He tried to deny these thoughts and convince himself, 'No, I am wrong here.' Shortly after that, his father returned home:

> Da heard he had been shot. He said to me that he thinks [name] is dead. He said, 'Don't say nothing to your mother. We are just going to have to tell your mother we think he was injured because we don't definitely know.' I was very sort of calm and eventually we got a lot of the people out of the house. Then my father told my mother and of course there was screaming and crying. There was younger sisters in the house, but we were clinging on to the hope, that maybe we were wrong. About ten minutes later one of the Knights of Malta [a voluntary ambulance service] came into the house and then it was confirmed that [name] was dead.

A young man, who at the 25th anniversary was the same age as his father when he was shot on Bloody Sunday, remembers how, as a six-year-old, he heard the news about his father's death from a playmate:

> I was playing with a young fella about the same age as myself, and after about ten or so minutes he just happened to say, 'Your father has been shot' as a matter of fact as that. I asked him how did he know and he said that he had been in Rossville Street, which was just a straight road

from our house and about a half-mile just straight up the
road. I didn't immediately believe what he was saying
although I had a niggling suspicion of it. I left him after ten
or 15 minutes. I probably went back to playing. I didn't
really understand the gravity of what had been said even
if it had been true.

He returned to his house and found his cousin there. She was a
distant cousin who lived nearby but rarely visited. He would not
have expected her to be there. She was in the kitchen, cleaning and
making tea. His anxiety increased at this unusual occurrence, but
the cousin ignored his questions:

> She was in the kitchen and I went out to the kitchen and
> asked her, 'Was my father shot?' and she wouldn't
> answer. I think at that stage I knew there was something
> badly wrong, but I didn't really tell anybody at least as
> far as I remember, nor did I pursue it any further. I just
> went back to the sitting room and I suppose just hoped
> against hope ... I suppose I thought if I told somebody at
> the time, it would probably be true. Sure enough, at
> about eight o'clock relatives all started landing to the
> house. At a later stage my mother told us just that my
> father had been killed.

Strong feelings including revenge, anger, fear and desire for retaliation are common responses in the aftermath of man-made
trauma (Gibson, 1996), emotions that deeply disturbed the traditional tight-knit fabric in many of the Bloody Sunday families. As
a family member related:

> It was not the same family after that. Well, we were never
> brought up to hate people who hated us, but we really did,
> we did. I remember telling one person, I feel I could shoot
> a soldier for my brother.

A family member, 16 years old at the time his brother was killed,
remembered, 'My immediate reaction was revenge or whatever,
illness, disbelief, a numbness, fear. I wanted to join the IRA.' His

response was typical of many young men in Derry, many of whom joined the IRA after Bloody Sunday (Taylor, 1997). Others confided they felt 'an awful lot of hatred' and 'anger' in the following days and months:

> I had it in my head that when 13 years had passed I was going to go and kill 13 paratroopers and let them know what it was for and go and kill 13 17-year-old sons belonging to them, or a 17-year-old brother belonging to them and let them know how we felt, how bad it was, how sore it was. I remember thinking something had to be done about [brother's name] way back then. I'm sure ten of us came out and joined the IRA, but one life by taking another is ... I probably would have been too scared anyway to join [the IRA], but then would that have been the right thing to do?

Going across to Altnagelvin

The nearest medical facility for casualties of the march was Altnagelvin Hospital on the other side of the River Foyle from where the shootings occurred. Someone from most of the families went to the hospital to determine if a family member was actually killed or just wounded. There was great confusion about what had happened. Crossing the Craigavon Bridge over the Foyle River to the hospital and identifying bodies was a harrowing and humiliating experience. Crisis management was non-existent. The perceived behaviour of the Royal Ulster Constabulary, the army, and the hospital staff added to a sense of powerlessness, a contributory factor in the aetiology of PTSD (Herman, 1992). The sister of a young man who was killed reported that when the police stopped her and her companions on the bridge, her boyfriend, an American sailor, told the RUC that they needed to go to the hospital. She remembered, 'The policeman laughed when my boyfriend told him we have to get through because there has been a member of my family killed, and the policeman was laughing. I seen him laughing a few times over the next few days.' She elaborated:

My brother was a boxer and quite a good one, actually, and they were taunting him about having killed his brother. He had to be held back. There was a good chance he would be hurt, badly hurt. He actually lost his rag [temper], you know. I think he would have fought. We just wanted to get to the hospital.

A brother of one of the dead was arrested while he and others were taking 'a wee boy to the hospital'. He didn't know at the time that his own brother was dead. They were stopped, 'dragged from the car and threw on the ground'. They tried to explain that they were taking the boy to the hospital, but they and the wounded boy were 'lying on the ground half an hour and they finally let us up, took us into the Saracen [armoured vehicle]. I don't know what they done to the boy.' The rest of them were handed over to the RUC, who then remanded them to the army at Ballykelly for interrogation. He continued:

When they took us into a cubicle, there was a chair in it. I sat down on it, and he pulled the chair out from under me. 'You're not supposed to sit on the chair. You're supposed to stand up with your face against the wall, stand against the wall.' I was to stand four or five hours, six hours.

The scene at the hospital was the antithesis of professional crisis management where relatives of victims encountered smirking soldiers, disrespect and chaos with 'all the paras [British Parachute Regiment] walking around with their rifles strutting, laughing, and carrying on. They didn't give a damn, to be truthful', the brother of a young man reported. A number of military vehicles were parked outside, and the Paras 'sneered at people' and searched them. Relatives were also greeted in the morgue by police and B Specials were armed with Sten guns. Family members went to the morgue where they found bodies lying on the floor and on trolleys, 'a terrible sight'. They searched among the dead, climbing over bodies without staff support until they found their dead relatives. No one had bothered to close eyes, and mouths were open. The father and the brother of a young man killed identified the body but were subjected to police scrutiny as they left the morgue:

On the way out, a cop stopped us. He said to my father, he said to all of us, 'Do you mind if I ask you a few questions?' and I told him to 'Fuck off!' Standing at the door, people crying, people under pressure, people in shock and they wanted to ask us questions and us trying to get away. 'Fuck away off', I said.

As they left the morgue, a Saracen arrived. They saw soldiers drag three bodies out of the Saracen and take them into Casualty, where they were pronounced dead. They roughly heaved the bodies into the Saracen and then drove away. The sister of one of the dead recalled her devastation when she heard what had happened to her brother's body, one of those taken away. Family members could not find the body. They made repeated trips to Altnagelvin, but the body was not there. A priest told her that her brother was dead and that the army had taken his body to the Foyle Road army post. The army held the body until late that night. Photographs later showed him in the back seat of a car with nail bombs jammed into his pockets. The sister was distraught at the violation of her brother's body and the assault on his integrity: 'It was bad enough them killing him, but planting the stuff was worse, that they could kill him and then take his body and plant these things on him.' She continued:

But the clothes that he wore was far too tight, so they couldn't even get the nail bombs into his clothes. You couldn't even hardly get your hand into his pocket because even the jacket that he had on him was very tight. There was only wee pockets. They would have had to open the jeans to put the nail bombs on him.

Traumatic stress and Bloody Sunday

The events of Bloody Sunday, we argue, were clearly terrifying and sufficient to cause PTSD as described by the *DSM-IV* (American Psychiatric Association, 1994: 425) system of classification: 'An event out of the range of ordinary human experience in which one's life or lives of one's family are endangered'. A family member recalled his terror at the traumatic event that is the significant marker in his life, regardless of other traumatic events in Northern Ireland. He believed his life was in grave danger:

> I will never forget that night. I don't think I was ever as afraid in my life before or since. It was just that one basic night. The whole thing was ... just the belief that it has happened and the word was coming out that there was two shot dead and there is three shot dead. Even at bedtime that night nobody knew the number of people that were dead. There was that many people had been shot, there was that many injured. What was the death toll going to be? Nobody knew. Was it going to stop? Was I going to be part of the death toll? They have gone mad altogether, they have just gone crazy!

Family members experienced many of the responses that characterise the stress response syndrome, a two-part cycle of denial and intrusions. The denial state occurs when the victim dismisses 'implications of threats or losses, forgets important problems, and experiences emotional numbing, withdrawal of interest in life, and behavioural constriction'. The intrusive state is characterised by 'unbidden ideas, sudden rushes of feeling, and even compulsive actions' (Horowitz, 1993: 50). During the denial phase the individual may stare off into space and avoid looking at others, including those who could be emotionally supportive. The person may narrowly focus on routine tasks in the immediate aftermath of crisis in an attempt to maintain a sense that life is unchanged. Inappropriate responses, such as going about routine tasks in the midst of the chaos in a robotic fashion are common. Bodily responses are diminished, the individual feels numb, perceptions are clouded, and the capacity to relate is impaired. Emotional blunting may impair interactions and result in the withdrawal of support systems just when they are most needed.

All of these responses were manifested in many of the Bloody Sunday family members' narratives which described the days immediately following their relatives' death. As they tried to cope with the horror of those deaths, the manner in which their relatives had died, and deal with funeral arrangements, denial was the predominant response. The day after Bloody Sunday, one man whose brother was killed, was dazed to the point of putting his own life in danger:

> I was walking down Westway. There was a gun battle on. The Provos [Provisional Irish Republican Army] had engaged the army. I remember seeing the tracer bullets. You would have seen them in the sky, ones that were not that high. They must have just either ricocheted or somehow found a stray path because they had to be from the army. I remember walking down and most times in the middle of a gun battle people will try and hide anywhere. I just didn't care. I just ... I walked on. I didn't bother. I was shattered.

The first few days after the killings was a 'terrible time' for all family members, yet in spite of the outpouring of condolences from friends and the community, family members felt isolated and could not relate to the support offered. It seemed as though 'literally thousands and thousands of people were coming through the house'. It was customary to greet people and make tea, accept condolences, but the pain was too great to relate to others:

> That house never emptied. It was the same as all the houses. It never emptied from morning to night. I mean it; at least to two, three or four in the morning. People was genuine. They were shocked and they wanted to express their condolences. At the time you felt isolated because there were that many people and you were trying to make them tea and thank them for calling, but you don't have time. The family is so ... they are caught in their own ways. My friends were coming talking to me and the sister's friends to her.
>
> I am there, supposed to be taking care of everybody but I give nobody a thought during those three days. Nobody. I never give nobody a thought. I don't know who was there. The neighbours was looking after things, you know and every time you wanted to cry you sort of just run into the bathroom. I was rushing in and out of there, crying and wiping my eyes and going back to the front door to greet

people. It was ludicrous. God, I couldn't think of anything worse, nothing worse has ever happened in my life and I hope it never does.

Describing the experience as a bad dream and 'feeling numb', 'a blur', and crying 'buckets of tears' were common themes poignantly illustrated in the family members' stories. Many of the details of the days immediately after Bloody Sunday were lost except for an awareness of people coming and going. One family member admitted that she made a conscious effort to 'lock it in the back' of her head, because if she could do this, 'it wasn't happening, it wasn't going on'. A sister of one of the dead tearfully related her painful experience:

> It was a ... a most horrible ... I don't know the feeling I had. There was just a lump, a lump all the time. I kept thinking 'Wake up, wake up, wake up!' I know I was saying that for about three days, at least three days. 'Wake up!' You often hear people saying it was like a bad dream, but I kept thinking, 'Please wake up, God wake me up. I want to wake up.' The pain was terrible, the pain was terrible.
>
> This is what it was like for me. Just a numbness. You walked about and you didn't want to speak to them, anybody at all, even your own particular family. You were just numb. There was nothing in your head, only this incident, this happening. You were just walking about more or less in a daze and you didn't really know them.

One young man had extreme difficulty believing that his brother was dead, and it was only when he awakened the next morning and heard his father crying that he became exquisitely aware of the reality of the death: 'My father crying, "Why didn't they wound him? They didn't have to kill him." That, that morning my father crying, is fixed in my head.'

Most of the family members reported memory gaps, 'blank memories', 'nothing'. One man cannot remember if he ever looked into the coffin to see his brother. He could not recall anything about the wake. Others concur that in between 'the chaos and sadness and tears and disbelief, crying, screaming and roaring and

[85]

whatever', they remembered an 'odd face', 'putting a lid on the coffin', 'putting a tricolour [Irish flag] in his coffin', 'being very calm', and 'my mother being devastated'. Some remember the death being confirmed and then nothing after that, others, 'the body being in the house, being in the chapel and walking behind a coffin'. One woman who came home from abroad for her brother's funeral was so dazed that she is still unable to recall how long she remained in Derry, a week, or two weeks. Still another didn't remember the funerals: 'I don't remember the Mass. I don't remember going up to St. Mary's to view the coffin or anything like that. I know I did do it. I think mostly it was blank in that respect. I know I was part of it.'

Denial is a normal human defence mechanism that allows a person to cope with stressful events and to break these events into manageable components. However, it becomes abnormal when a person avoids the stressors to such an extent that he or she does not deal with them at all. The individual may substitute other means of coping such as alcohol, drugs or risky behaviour, or frantic increases in activity like sports, work or sexual activity. These behaviours help stifle emotions and block thoughts about the trauma. Some factors that may affect how a person responds to trauma and to whom the person expresses the resultant emotions include personality type, culture, and a person's habitual way of making sense of stressful events.

Some family members, especially the men and boys, felt they needed to be emotionally strong for the rest of the family and 'keep things going' because parents were too traumatised to function. One man remembered he 'only cried once' in the bathroom where he had locked the door. He felt that he 'maybe had to be the person who had to be the strongest' because his sisters 'couldn't handle it. My mother couldn't handle it. My Da was too busy trying to kill it, kill the emotion of it with a bottle. So we had to make our arrangements.'

The funerals: 'Thirteen coffins ... a side show'

A funeral is a very important ritual that can help in resolving grief (Pynoos, 1985). In traumatic deaths, funerals and wakes are often not normal. Going to the chapel was a 'terrible time' for family members with mothers hanging out car windows, 'roaring and squealing and crying'. A common reaction to the funeral itself among family members who were adolescents or younger at the time 'was just the crowd and the numbness and the saddest thing you ever seen'. The city was at a standstill, the 'unbelievable crowds' stood silent in torrential rains, on cars, on rooftops on that 'wild, wet, dirty day'. A sister of one of the dead, who was 13 at the time, was terrified. The sight of 13 coffins along the front of the chapel confused her because she had 'never seen anything like that before, not even a dead body'.

A recurring theme among family members was that the funeral was taken away from them by visiting clergy and political dignitaries, the media hype, and the sheer size of the crowds which prevented them from following their own relative's funeral procession. Many of them felt left out of the funeral and deprived of the personal experience of private family grieving. One family member remembered feeling furious when someone at the door of the church demanded that he present a ticket for admission to the funeral service:

> They weren't getting no ticket from me. We were chauffeured over to the side. All the front of the church were kept for all these bishops and archbishops and MPs [Members of Parliament]. I did not think that was very fair. Reporters and photographers walking around the altar rails and the lights were up. It was a total sham. I wasn't a part of the Mass for my brother. We had nothing to do with it. We were part of a side show.

Intrusive thoughts about Bloody Sunday came later and were bothersome for many family members at certain times, particularly anniversaries (Horowitz, 1997). Intrusions include nightmares, flashbacks, and compulsive ruminations about the event, those that preceded it or occurred later, or about events remotely associated with the trauma. Intrusive phases often consist of mentally re-enacting the event and people may assume an active role, rather than the passive, powerless role that may have been the reality. Intrusions and denial alternate in cycles and generally diminish with time.

A family member acknowledged that at certain times of the year, if there is a resumption of violence, Bloody Sunday is her only conversation and she finds it very difficult to concentrate on other matters. For her, it is difficult to 'get out of bed in the morning, get through the day, a constant fight'. Memory lapses were a problem for her: 'You can't hold a conversation because you can't remember what you have just said a minute ago. You need reminders all the time. My brain feels as if it has scattered everywhere because it certainly is not in the one place any more.' She has difficulty watching news or reading newspapers because it would 'get' to her. She continued:

> It is in my head all the time. Whenever I start talking, I get carried away. I forget to stop. I can't stop it. That will go on and it will be February or March. There is a pattern coming up to Christmas. I get kind of anxious. This is the time when I am beginning to go down hill because I know what is coming right after it. The tension is beginning to build and then we are into January and I eat, sleep and breathe Bloody Sunday.

During an intrusive phase, the individual may be hyper-vigilant or excessively alert. This state renders individuals acutely sensitive to any stimuli regardless of how innocuous, especially stimuli associated with the traumatic event, for example, a loud noise that sounds like gunfire. Other examples of this state include muscle tension or assuming a protective stance as if warding off an attack, or taking cover. In the intrusive state, an individual may experience pseudo-hallucinations and may see or feel the presence of those who were killed during the traumatic event. This is particularly anxiety and fear provoking since it tends to occur prior to falling asleep. People can feel out of control and this is worse for those whose prolonged denial lulled them into believing recovery from the trauma had occurred.

One family member, an adolescent at the time of Bloody Sunday, talked about the difficulties he and his family had in accepting the reality of his father's death. Because of the extent of the victim's injuries, the coffin was closed, preventing the normal funeral ritual and interfering with the process of grief work in a traumatised family (Pynoos, 1985). Nightmares, a form of intrusive recollections (American Psychiatric Association, 1994), were a problem and there was nowhere to get help:

> So, where all the other families had the coffin open and they could actually see that the person was dead, we had the wake but it was a box. Nightmares, in my dream he was there. The last time we'd seen him he was alive and we hadn't seen him in his dying state, and I found it extremely difficult to accept.

Horowitz (1997) alludes to pseudo-hallucinations commonly experienced during the intrusive phase. The childhood memories of a family member focus on the smell of his brother's wake. This has never left him, suggesting an olfactory traumatic memory and perhaps a pseudo-hallucination that is triggered at other wakes. He remembers his brother's body being in the house and asking his father about a smell he noticed. His father told him that it was a 'death smell, because of the bullets' that went into his brother's body. He added, 'I wouldn't say it would be a bad smell, but it wasn't a nice smell. I always mind that smell. That smell always stayed with me. I always mind that when I went into a wake after, years after it, and I was expecting to smell the death.'

Another family member described his experience with auditory hallucinations. These continue to occur after 25 years. He asserted that the memories of that terrible time will never leave him, because 'It's just in your head and it's going to stay there. For instance now, you could even hear the shots in your own head, hear them.'

Foreshortened life and survivor guilt

Traumatised individuals may have a sense of foreshortened future [not expecting to have a career, marriage, children, or a normal life span (American Psychiatric Association, 1994: 425)]. Three members of the same family recalled a story about their brother who was in trouble for under-age drinking. His death put this episode and teen drinking into perspective for them. A small enjoyment, they concluded, because life is short and 'after all, it wasn't the drink that killed him'. For another man his brother's death influenced his decision to marry early:

> He died at 17 in 1972. When I was 17, and this country was the way it was, we decided we were getting married. I got married and I was 17 years of age and he died at that age. People were saying to me, 'Do you know what you are doing?' and all the rest of it, but I said, 'I could be where he is. I could be dead. I am doing what I want to do.' Life is short. My older brother is no longer there and this [getting married] cannot be as bad or as dangerous as whatever life was going to throw you.

Individuals with posttraumatic stress disorder may describe 'painful guilt feelings about surviving when others did not survive' (American Psychiatric Association, 1994: 425). Survivor guilt was clearly apparent in many of the interviews. Some family members, remembering their unease prior to the march, expressed a sense of responsibility for the deaths of their brothers as one family member explained: 'If I had have been a bit more forceful and talked everybody into staying here, maybe I could have changed some of the events that day', or, he added, 'Things might have turned out differently. In that sense I feel guilt.' Another man tearfully recalled his dilemma about telling his family about what happened at the march and invoked his dead brother: 'I didn't know how I was going to tell them, look at them and say I was ...' He trailed off. He then called out to his dead brother '[brother's name] if I ...' He despaired that he had not done more to prevent the tragedy and then continued: 'If I had went on, I would have got him.'

Another man felt he should have waited a bit longer before running away from the soldiers: 'Maybe if I had been with him ... how did I not see him in Glenfadda Park?' As another man told his story, he wept and he too, called out to his dead brother, 'You silly bastard you, why were you there? What were you doing? You shouldn't have been, but I was there and we were brothers.' Had he been with his brother, he might have done something to prevent his death.

[90]

Working through trauma

Unassimilated traumatic experiences are stored in what Horowitz (1997) refers to as 'active memory', accounting for the cycles of denial and intrusions with nightmares, flashbacks and the need to re-enact the trauma. This process continues until the person develops a new mental schema, either positive or negative, to explain what has happened. The sister of a young man killed on Bloody Sunday developed a schema to encompass traumatic memories in her now changed world:

> I have no trust. It has totally killed my trust in human nature. For instance, when I meet somebody for the first time, I mean, you might decide to yourself, 'Well, that's a nice person', but I always think in terms of 'She *seems* like a nice person. He *seems* like a nice person', not 'They are a nice person.' Always a little doubt there. As for soldiers and policemen, I know I would never ever trust the forces, never, ever.

Working through trauma, accomplished in small doses, cognitively and emotionally, leads to the fading of trauma symptoms over time, but symptoms can return years later through reminders of the painful event. When a traumatic event results in a violent death of a loved one, the process of bereavement is held in abeyance until the trauma in worked through (Dillenburger, 1994; Pynoos, 1985). For example, after 25 years a frequent comment expressed by some Bloody Sunday family members was that they have not yet begun to grieve the death of their sibling or parent:

> It's not very easy to talk about a family member who has been murdered. I never, ever felt comfortable about it because there was nothing final. It's never been laid to rest. It will never be stopped. If you could talk about it, when it hasn't ended. ... It's easier to talk when everything's settled until finally somebody came out and said all them people were innocent. Then we could sit and talk about it and then we'd say, 'Well, what was he really

like?' and various things like that. 'Well, what did he actually do?' and you can just get on with it. There is no pain involved with it. Well, the pain is still involved like, but it's over so you can just sit and talk.

If a person continues to live in a threatening situation that does not allow access to the memory and the opportunity to relate the memory in narrative form is not possible, then the trauma is less likely to be processed. The probability that chronic PTSD will develop increases (Hunt, 1997). In Derry, the events of Bloody Sunday shattered trust in the peacekeeping force and left many people silent and with a profound sense of injustice and powerlessness, not unlike that of a child abused by a parent. Furthermore, the trauma was compounded by constant reminders of the event in the media, troops on the streets of Derry, and army house raids targeting Bloody Sunday families. Family members felt they were 'harassed by the security forces to a terrible degree, as if we were the perpetrators. Instead of being the innocent we were guilty, we were responsible for Bloody Sunday.'

A family member recalled:

> being picked up and getting threw into an army land rover [military vehicle] and being held until 5 o'clock in the morning. I have also had soldiers come in and raided my house knowing who I was and then driving past me in the street and saying 'Hello [name]'. What sort of impression does that leave on people when the British army are greeting you?

His mother and sisters were arrested and held for interrogation in the weeks following Bloody Sunday. House raids were extremely upsetting for him and frightening for his children as soldiers barged into the house at night 'dove up the stairs and got everybody out of their beds'. His older son, a baby at the time, was terrified when he woke to see 'a soldier hanging from the loft' on his way to the downstairs area. Nightmares were always a problem after raids.

[92]

Summary

In this chapter, we presented family members' reflections and perspectives about the event of Bloody Sunday. The narratives portrayed the human experience of trauma. Many family members displayed classic symptoms of PTSD. From the moments when the violence began, in the midst of the killings and during the traumatic aftermath of the day, many respondents struggled with denial, intrusive thoughts and complex emotions of grief, disbelief and anger. They continue to suffer the painful effects of trauma over a quarter of a century later.

There were no models for crisis intervention available to Bloody Sunday family members in 1972 and for many years later. Relief of pain associated with the trauma was achieved through prescription of sedatives or self-medication with alcohol. There was no assistance for families who were treated by police and the military with disdain. Many family members reported being jeered at, taunted, and they witnessed dead bodies being handled disrespectfully. Wakes and funerals took place in an atmosphere of chaos, confusion, and dismissal of family needs, so the ritual of the funeral was not useful in helping to bring closure to the trauma. Fear of repercussions and harassment by police and the military made seeking help impossible and engendered a culture of silence for many years. Grief, bereavement and working through the trauma were held in abeyance and continue to be unresolved for many family members. Schemas formed in attempts to make sense of the trauma reflect a keen sense of distrust.

6 The traumatic aftermath

Given the extent of the violence which occurred on Bloody Sunday, we were interested in how such a catastrophic event affected the lives of the siblings and children of those killed, the human experience of trauma. The words of the Bloody Sunday family members, we believe, are living testimony to the significance of that event for them. Their narratives of grief, mourning and healing illustrate theoretical perspectives presented earlier in this work (Garbarino, Kostelny and DuBrow, 1991; Herman, 1992; Pynoos, 1985). The interviews revealed intense loss, the pain of living with a traumatised parent, anger and the need for justice, and the development of values which became important to these family members years later in rearing their own children. A strong anti-violent, apolitical philosophy evolved as a protective mechanism for many family members, a shield against further loss.

Parents taught their children that there were other ways to conduct themselves in human interactions (Garbarino, Kostelny and DuBrow, 1991). Parents sometimes offered themselves as role models in dealing with volatile situations. The data which emerged from this study suggest that, overall, the Bloody Sunday family member participants who were children, adolescents or young adults at the time of the event, have instilled tolerance for group differences and respect for human life in their children as a way to insure against further loss.

Trauma, grief and loss

The stories of the Bloody Sunday families poignantly illustrate the differences between grief and bereavement, and grief complicated by trauma (Dillenburger, 1992; Horowitz, 1993; Pynoos, 1985). The loss of a relative was markedly different from family deaths that occurred under 'normal' circumstances. A family member who had experienced many losses pointedly explained the differences:

> I think about my mother, and her only dead six months. I think about my father and my brothers and my young

sister, but we don't talk about my mother's death or my
father's death, or my brothers' death, because it wasn't a
tragedy. It was horrible at the time, but it wasn't a tragedy,
where [name]'s death was a tragedy. You can accept a
natural death but you can't accept an unnatural one.

Other family members also felt that they could accept the death of
relatives when it seemed like a natural occurrence, but, as many
stated, the deaths of those who died on Bloody Sunday were
unjust and the effects somehow more long lasting. Expressions
such as it 'never should have happened', and 'it is like a thing
that's going to stick with us forever' were common.

Family members were also affected by maternal dysfunction
following Bloody Sunday. A stable relationship with at least one
parent, particularly with one's mother and continuity of family
routines is important following a trauma (Blease, 1983;
Garbarino, Kostelny and DuBrow, 1991), however, one mother
could not leave the house in the days and weeks after Bloody
Sunday because she wanted to avoid everyone and everything
that could remind her of the death of her son. Her children
followed her example. Her daughter recalled, 'You just couldn't
cope with it. You just didn't want to talk. We were just sitting
round. You just didn't want to know. You want to hide and not
go out. It was terrifying.' Members of this family did not want to
return to work and felt they could not bear to accept condolences. Months later, when the mother first ventured out of the
house, many people who had not seen her since her son's death
expressed sympathy. This was so upsetting that her daughters
immediately brought their distraught mother home. Her
emotional state continued to deteriorate and she could not dress
herself. She began to sleep in her daughter's room.

The brother of a young man killed described his mother as
emotionally dead following Bloody Sunday. She suffered from a
'broken heart', and was a 'completely different' woman. He closed
his eyes and moved his head from side to side repeatedly as he
told the story:

Nothing worse has ever happened in my life, I know that,
but watching my mother. ... That particular day, if they

had've shot my mother they would have done her a favour. He was the youngest of the whole lot of us. He was only 17, the only one left at home. Everybody else was married. So, as I say, they might as well have shot my mother that day too because she more or less died on the scene. So that date for her, no matter how many times, ten years later, twelve years later, if you were in the house at that time she was crying.

Another mother 'never wanted to live after Bloody Sunday'. Her daughter recalled sadly, 'When my mother was dying the only thing she had to do to live was to eat, but my mother would not eat because she didn't want to live. Her spirit was broken.' In yet another family, the mother never recovered from the trauma of Bloody Sunday. Her son explained, 'The trauma of the whole occasion for her was quite debilitating in terms of other relationships, problem solving and so on.'

The children of those killed were profoundly affected by the violent death of their parents. They had to take on adult roles in the family very early. One became the 'problem solver within the household'. Another family member said that he changed from a boy to a man within 24 hours after his father's death:

> They say that God has no greater gift, or a man has no greater gift than to lay down his life for a friend but when I looked at it at the time I was 16 and a half, so there were five kids younger than me and so it totally devastated our lives. We depended so much on him. People said to me, 'It was a very difficult time that you came through.' It was a very difficult life. Our loss was tremendous and we still feel it to this day.

In another family the mother also became the paramount concern whilst the father coped with alcohol. One of her sons sadly reflected, his father 'went and got a pint' but as far as his mother was concerned, 'A link was taken out of the chain' when her youngest son died. The mother's behaviour became increasingly erratic. The losses the family suffered have made him determined he said passionately, 'to rectify the unjustness of

Bloody Sunday. I live and breathe Bloody Sunday. It's as simple as that.' The children in this family felt obliged to follow their mother when she left the house because her behaviour was so unpredictable. She was missing one day and they found her 'roaring at the Brits about killing her son'. One time she became hysterical when she noticed that her son's grave had settled. She thought that the grave was moving. Sometimes she and the mother of another young man killed sat in the cemetery 'chatting at the wall'. Her children found her lying on top of the grave with a blanket in the wintertime, trying to keep her dead son warm. She kept the dead youth's clothes and they will be buried with her when she dies along with a Mars bar [chocolate bar] which he had in his pocket when he died.

For all family members, 'things were never the same' after Bloody Sunday. Their inconsolable losses extended beyond the death of a loved one and permeated all aspects of their lives. Their losses are still felt today, the depth of the loss unchanged as part of their incomplete grieving process. Important rituals could not be celebrated in the aftermath of Bloody Sunday, a profound loss in a community with strong family bonds. One man whose wedding was on the eve of Bloody Sunday admitted guiltily that he never offered or even thought about offering his wife a proper honeymoon or a proper anniversary. Sadly, what should have been the joyful occasion of his 25th wedding anniversary could not be celebrated either. Another man whose father was killed remembered the first Christmas after Bloody Sunday:

> Christmas was a great time in our house because he was really a Christmas-time person. Everything was being focused or geared to the family. On that particular Christmas day, I remember it well. It was like the world ended. We sat on the bed, my mum was sitting on the bed with six of us round her, and that was it, sitting and crying.

For others, there was a great big 'aching hole' left in their hearts, a profound sense of loss for what might have been. As he wondered what life would have been like had his brother lived, a family member sobbed:

[97]

If only he was here. He was a year older. You look up to
your big brother and you show off to your big brother. I
would want him to see my wife and my weans [children].
It is not there you know. It is gone. I feel terrible. I
wonder would he have married and where would he be
working and what would his weans [children] be like?
Did he stick to the football? What would it have been
like? You'll never know. Even with such a big family you
would think it doesn't matter. There is only one missing,
but it's not like that.

Several family members agreed that 'it wasn't just the dead on
Bloody Sunday, but their children were lost as well, maybe a
hundred. So you're talking about a generation being lost too,
within those 13 people.' They felt a generation was 'taken off the
face of the earth because of the pigs that came along'. The tragedy
of Bloody Sunday affected many more family members than those
represented in this study sample, and people in the wider community as well. A family member asserted the soldier who killed his
brother 'didn't only affect the one person, he affected hundreds
and hundreds of people, just in my own family alone. They may
have shot one person but they done a lot of damage to a lot of
people just with that one particular person.' Another family
member offered an additional insight that illustrates the magnitude of the event and underscored the argument that Bloody
Sunday had 'seismic' consequences for that generation of Derry
youth (Taylor, 1997: 127):

I think it goes deeper than just the people that were shot
dead on Bloody Sunday and the follow-up to Bloody
Sunday. I would still maintain that there were hundreds of
people lost their lives and thousands injured because of
Bloody Sunday. A lot of people would still be alive today
if Bloody Sunday hadn't have happened.

The loss of one's personal identity to that of being a Bloody
Sunday family member was another consequence of the event. A
child of a man killed reported that 'It was part of your life really.
Derry is a small town and there was no escaping from that as a

teenager. You grow up in the Bogside. You're in the midst of the area in which it took place.' His first experience of being seen as somebody associated with the killings rather than an individual, was when he went to a shop to buy something for his mother. The grocer's wife whispered to her husband, 'That's that wee boy [family name] whose father died on Bloody Sunday'. The grocer gave him his bread and did not charge him for it. From that day on, he knew he would always be seen as someone associated with a 'very, very black event' in the history of the city. For years, he recalled, 'I was introduced as somebody's son rather than [name] who works in such in such or who is married to such and such.'

Other losses directly attributed to Bloody Sunday included a 13-year-old girl's loss of confidence that she attributed to loss of parental support after Bloody Sunday. Before the event she recalled being a very secure, confident person, 'with no worries or problems'. Overnight her parents changed, leaving her feeling very insecure:

> They had turned into angry, bitter people. I actually witnessed my mother being violent to soldiers. I never did see violence at home and I began to feel it emotionally, my mother being violent and angry words. I didn't see this before.

Another family member reported loss of religious faith, an associated feature of PTSD (American Psychiatric Association, 1994). The way he and his family were treated on the day of the funeral caused him at age 16 to 'fall out with the Catholic church'. He found it extremely unfair that he and his family were not able to be more of a part of the funeral for his dead brother. He felt their participation had been denied by the press, by politicians, and especially by the clergy.

'We don't talk about it'

Many participants provided descriptions of their experiences and perceptions of Bloody Sunday for the first time during the present study. Relatives did not know some of the details of their other siblings' experiences before the interviews conducted by Patrick

Hayes. One reason for this is the degree of pain it might have caused in families. As one woman remarked, 'We would all end up crying. So to be honest when we are all together, we don't talk a great deal about it.' The relative lack of narrative on this subject was evident in many accounts: 'We don't talk about it. We don't', 'I remember the hurt. If I don't talk about it, it's not there', 'I think if I don't talk about it, it never happened', 'It's hurting me. I don't want to talk about it'. One family member said, however, they do talk about it, but when they do, they 'have talked about the anger, a lot of anger'.

Anger: 'They were innocent ... Have to get a fair hearing'

The need for justice is an important element in trauma integration and completion of the grieving process (Herman, 1992). The respondents tended to share a strong sense of injustice, mistrust of the British government, and a belief that someone should take responsibility for what happened on Bloody Sunday. The families wanted the government to 'come clean', to exonerate the victims who were labelled as 'bombers and gunmen'. One woman was incredulous that her brother was named as a terrorist because 'you would not be going out to shoot a gun or riot in a three-piece suit'. She forcefully asserted his innocence and lamented the loss of life 'for somebody so young and the way it was done. It was a rotten thing for a government to do or for whoever set it up.' Others had similar thoughts and called for governmental acknowledgment of injustice and wrongful death, along with accountability for those involved, as this sister of a young man killed argued:

> My attitude has always been that the perpetrators should be brought to justice all the way up to the Prime Minister, not just the soldier that pulled the trigger. I feel they should be brought to book and should pay in some way for what they did. I mean they slaughtered 13 innocent people and tried to actually kill quite a few more. Ted Heath [the Prime Minister at the time of Bloody Sunday]... Lord Widgery [the judge who chaired the Widgery Tribunal], I feel he should, well, he is dead now, so he can't be, but I feel his family should feel the shame. They should feel the shame of what he did.

Some family members have become angry as they 'became aware of what really happened'. They become upset when people say 'Put the past in the past.' 'We have not begun to deal with it, never mind to put it in the past.' As one woman added, 'the insulting goes on year in and year out' particularly victim blaming:

> You know it wasn't bad enough that they killed him. They made it worse by saying that he could have been in prox-imity to someone who was shooting or doing this or he could have been doing that earlier. I understand their reason for it because it's part of their cover up. ... When you try to work your way through that it's very, very diffi-cult. I mean there are times even now that they will turn round and say things like 'the Bloody Sunday ones deserved what they got'.

One family member would channel his anger differently now than he would have in the past, perhaps to the 'soldier who actually pulled the trigger, the person that gave him the order to do it, the politician who said it was OK, and the judge who covered it up, and the politicians since who have covered it up'. Family members' anger after Bloody Sunday was directed initially towards revenge, but this eventually evolved into a movement to seek justice from within the system because, as one family member said, 'Until the British government says that they done wrong, it will always remain a tragedy both in our household and every other household.'

Family members railed about their perceptions of injustice at the hands of the Widgery Tribunal. Respondents thought it was 'a sham from the beginning, not impartial, not fair'. As far as they were concerned, 'The Coroner Major said it was murder. Should somebody not have been tried for that? After all, they had soldiers who admitted that they fired the bullet that shot him.' Others felt there was no need to confront the government. Justice would be served eventually. As one woman said, 'The guilty ones, at the end of the day, will have to meet their maker.' Another man asserted, 'We don't need the British Government to tell us he was innocent. Let them rest in peace. We know they are innocent. I don't think their names need clearing.' One family member angrily retorted, 'I have no time for British justice because the two words are incompatible and do not belong in the same dictionary!'

Family members often predicted intergenerational consequences of this perceived perpetuation of injustice that will result in a continuation of the violence in Northern Ireland:

> Those people responsible have to own up that they did something wrong. As long as they don't admit that, this is going to go on. It will probably pass to another generation. Listen to my nieces and nephews, they take a Republican side.

The Bloody Sunday Justice Campaign: 'I thought I could do something'

While not all family members felt the need to confront the government, as the previous narratives suggest, many do want the government to apologise. In the meantime, a number found the Campaign to be a source of support for 'those who suffered the same thing on the same day, in a 20 minute period'. It is 'like a therapy', a way to talk about things, decrease distress, learn facts and share painful experiences with others. A family member who has benefited from her work with the Campaign diligently educated herself about Bloody Sunday. She has succeeded in confronting her pain: 'I can bring it back into my mind where I had it buried deep. I found the more and more I talk about it, the easier it is to cope with it'. Bitter, angry or hurt family members decided they could do something about having their relatives' name cleared, fully exonerated. They wanted 'everyone to know they are innocent and want the whole world and its mother to know the truth ... to have that stigma taken away because even though it is 25 years, they are still classed as bombers and gunmen'. Other family members felt that it helped to manage their anger by trying to campaign for a declaration of innocence for those killed and to place the blame for the killings on those responsible (Herman, 1992):

> That has been over 25 years and to think that some of the people we are fighting for only walked this earth for 17

years. The campaign has actually been going on for longer
than he lived. I find that to be heart wrecking. I feel terrible that there is no more that we can do for him. In the end
it is up to the British government to put their hand up and
say, 'Sorry, we are guilty.' They are guilty because it was
definitely planned.

Another woman, an expatriate for many years, returned to Derry
and joined the Campaign. Since she had not been home during the
years when her brother was growing up, she admits to many years
of doubting his innocence. However, she felt that she now needed
to know the truth:

I didn't know him, so how could I know? So I suppose as
things came out about these instances with the Birmingham Six and the Guildford Four [cases of miscarriages of
justice against Irish people in Britain] and this, where you
really begin to distrust the authorities then.... Well, my
parents always believed he's totally innocent. I began to
think that maybe he was. Like, maybe the British brain-
washed me, enough to create some doubts. I personally
would like a new inquiry so that I would know the truth,
no matter what that truth is.

Anti-violence and apoliticism: protecting the next generation

The pain of loss deeply influenced family members' thinking
about violence and politics. With a few exceptions, the siblings
and children of the men killed on Bloody Sunday became parents
who developed an apolitical stance and a passionate ethic for
anti-violence, a mechanism that served to protect their children
and to shield themselves from further loss. A few leaned towards
the Republican side of the conflict in Northern Ireland, but they
were aware they might transmit attitudes that could foster anger
and 'thoughts of retribution', that would 'bring more pain into
the house and suffering', so they were very careful about
discussing political issues with their children. Many family
members seemed to have an intuitive understanding that their
children were vulnerable to persuasion to join political factions

[103]

that could place them in harm's way. Family members tended to equate political activity and sectarianism with violence, so heated discussions that might reveal parental anger, sadness, or bitterness, or transmit attitudes that could evoke a violent response from children were avoided. As a family member said, 'Yes, I want a united Ireland, yes, I want freedom, yes, I don't like British rule, but there is no way I am going to die for it and I don't want my children to die for it.'

A few family members, however, expressed ambivalence about the use of violence. As one put it: 'There are a lot of pacifists at the present time, and it's great to condemn violence, but to condemn it without an alternative ... ?' One man wished that the killer of his father would lose his own son and another family member thought there were times when he would have liked to face the soldier who killed his brother, but he is relieved, however, that the opportunity has not presented itself. He fears the consequences of his anger: 'I could kill a man if he came out with a point-blank statement that they [those killed] were all gunmen, I think I would kill him.' The thought of losing another family member to violence or inflicting that kind of pain on someone else was, however, for most family members, unacceptable.

Most family members could not tolerate the thought that anyone else should feel the kind of pain they felt, because as one woman believed, 'in my enemy there is something there that other people see that is attractive'. They generally disagreed with the notion of retaliatory violence. One respondent described her feelings in the context of the conflict in Northern Ireland. She acknowledged that Catholics and Protestants who had lost a family member suffered equally:

> Regardless of who killed their son or daughter, I wouldn't want them to go through what we went through. I can't come to terms with anything that the IRA did in the name of it, because somebody's brother or sister must suffer for it. Not just for the Nationalist side of it or the Unionist side, because at the end of the day, they lost sons and daughters as well.

Another family member who disagreed with 'any kind of violence being inflicted on anybody' was also admittedly not politically aware [taking a side in the political struggles of the day] and, she asserted, 'I don't want to be either. The only thing I know about is Bloody Sunday. I have watched too many people join the IRA and they are destroying themselves.' Another was concerned about being too easily identified with ideologies which she shunned:

> The IRA were doing this and that in the name of Bloody Sunday. They were inclined to desecrate the deaths. They couldn't undo what was done. Hurting somebody else didn't make it any easier for us. I don't agree with the British Government or the army, and I can't agree with what they [the IRA] were doing either.

Her anti-violent stance defined the way she role-modelled for her children (Garbarino, Kostelny and DuBrow, 1991). The event had changed her way of thinking: 'Even when the police has done something or maybe said something to make me angry in the presence of my children, I would not react when my children were there.' Another family member spoke admiringly of his mother who was widowed on Bloody Sunday:

> My mother was 39 years of age with six kids, bringing them up in Northern Ireland in Derry, background of violence and everything else. She didn't let us have any sort of hatred or breed hatred or anything like that. She took us past that.

His mother was 'a pretty strong woman with a great belief in God and in us'. She took on the role of mother and father, and she was not going to risk losing any more of her family to violence:

> I was 16 and a half and obviously my first feelings were of revenge but that was never to be. My mother, on the exact same day that my father was killed made me get down in front of her and the holy picture and she made me swear that I would never get involved in anything. I would never

do the same type of thing that those people had done to her. I swore that I would never become involved in anything [paramilitary violence] and I never did.

Some family members included a non-sectarian education and exposure to 'other ideas' (Garbarino, Kostelny and DuBrow, 1991). One woman explained, 'I have made a conscious attempt to reverse. I didn't know any Protestants when I was growing up, I didn't know what the Protestant culture was. I didn't know anything about them.' Another woman not only taught her children that 'violence is immoral', but also expressed a belief in the senseless of violence because 'it doesn't resolve the situation because no matter, eventually you will lose'. An alternative approach was to develop an attitude of forgiveness:

> I know that my mother always said, if she ever seen the soldier that killed him, she would forgive him. I would never have thought like that until they [her own children] started growing up. If the soldier that killed him was in front of me tonight and said to me, 'I killed your brother, I murdered him', I think my first reaction would be to hit him, but I would forgive him. I would forgive him. I couldn't have said that 20 years ago but now that I have family, I would never want the children to go out and hurt anyone, and I would never want anyone to hurt them.

Many participants also protected their children by not allowing them to go on marches or participate in demonstrations, fearful of violence, and that the children would become politically minded, a constant worry:

> Up until that day, people would've said, 'Ach, that wouldn't happen', but it happened. So the same thing could happen again just as easily as it happened then. It could just happen to this family again just as easily as any other family. Hopefully, we've kept it all away from them political-wise because none of them at all would be politically minded, none of them. They're of an age now, obviously when they

can make up their own mind but they're still not politically minded, so that helps.

Most family members told their children very little about Bloody Sunday and some made a deliberate effort not to tell the children anything in another effort to protect them from violence. Several waited to tell the story until the children were older. Family members equated knowledge about Bloody Sunday with the potential for transmitting political attitudes that could lead to life-threatening political activity, particularly joining the IRA. One mother, however, told her children the story of Bloody Sunday around the time of the hunger strikes [this led to the deaths of Republican prisoners who were protesting against their treatment in jail]. She feared they were becoming habituated to violence in the community (Toner, 1994) and telling them the story of Bloody Sunday was her way of protecting them. On a particularly troublesome night in Derry, the children could not understand why their mother would not allow them '... to store petrol in our back yard'. The children couldn't understand why they couldn't be out rioting like everyone else, '... lifting up sidewalks and breaking them to throw as ammunition against soldiers'. She 'sat them down' and explained:

> 'Listen, if you get into trouble, things can happen, being in the wrong place at the wrong time, and it cost [brother's name] his life.' I never wanted to lose anybody over the bother. I was trying to make sure it wouldn't happen to any of mine.

Concern that the children would become 'bitter' was a common theme among the family members who didn't tell their children about what happened on Bloody Sunday. They 'didn't want to teach hate ... if you carry hatred with you it will eat into your soul and make you bitter.' One man was concerned that his potentially homicidal anger and ambivalence about killing would infect his children. Another family member wanted to protect her daughter 'from as much as I can. I try to bring her up properly to like people, not judge.' One mother told her son nothing because, 'I suppose I don't want him to be sad. I don't want him to be sad about anything. I don't want there to be any hurt there.'

Summary

This chapter presented narrative material which describes in their own words how family members experienced the aftermath of traumatic loss. While the loss of the siblings and children of the men killed was immeasurable, leading to many as yet unresolved emotions and thoughts about the past, present and the future, many relatives appeared to try to instil strong values of anti-violence and apoliticism in the next generation. We believe this might be viewed as a protective mechanism against further loss. Nonetheless, a great deal of anger and pain about unresolved issues associated with the injustices surrounding Bloody Sunday remain. The Bloody Sunday Justice Campaign was one way to deal with the trauma, but this occurred years later.

7 State and community responses to trauma

In previous chapters we have described and analysed a variety of themes which help explain the events of Bloody Sunday and how they may have impacted on family members. International research suggests that how the state and the wider community respond to such events may be of significance in terms of trauma resolution (Hough and Vega, 1990; Ayalon and Soskis, 1986; Swartz, 1998). The following chapter tracks the development of health and social care services developed during the Troubles, and critically assesses the manner in which they were organised and delivered over this 35-year period. The factors that influenced the development of services are important in terms of understanding the needs of the families and wider Derry community following Bloody Sunday. It is difficult to be precise about the impact of such violence, but when one considers the size of families in Derry over 30 years ago (for example, one family in the present study had 15 children and many had more than ten children), the 'ripple effect' must have been substantial.

A critical examination of the history of service delivery to victims of the Troubles, such as the families of people who lost their lives on Bloody Sunday, suggests a story of piecemeal organisational arrangements, shaped by the social divisions in Northern Ireland, failures in political processes and the operation of professional ideologies that tended to limit opportunities for Troubles-related interventions. Bloody Sunday was a violent incident that, like many others in Northern Ireland, left unresolved issues of grief and trauma for individuals, families and whole communities. Excerpts from interviews carried out five years after the original study suggest that this group, historically, have had little opportunity to access services. The chapter concludes with a discussion about how recent developments in the field of trauma response may offer new types of interventions which could help deal with at least some of the pain experienced by the families. Nevertheless, the problematic issue of victimhood and the difficulties in providing resources and constructing services which are flexible enough to meet the competing needs of such a diverse population are real and as yet unresolved.

The early period of the Troubles

Any examination of the way in which health and social care agencies and professionals responded to the political violence of the Troubles is incomplete without some understanding of the role of the state in managing the conflict. In the first few years of the conflict (1968–72) the existing systems of health and social welfare were ill-equipped to deal with escalating levels of political and inter-communal violence. Northern Ireland was a small, somewhat marginal provincial region with services funded for peace and not civil and political violence. The eruption of street violence and its consequent impact on the social and economic fabric of the region left many professionals and agencies trying to manage as best they could. For example the inter-communal violence which characterised life in the interface areas of Belfast during this early period led to the greatest shift of civilian population in western Europe since the Second World War; this in a province of only 1.6 million people. Housing, income maintenance, and health and social welfare resources were stretched to the limits as the local state struggled to address need. In health care settings doctors and nurses were faced with the aftermath of widespread bombings and shootings that left thousands of people physically injured and psychologically scarred. Social care staff often had to be flexible about their use of social assistance and sometimes were obliged to negotiate access to communities through discussions with paramilitary groups. These sudden changes in the way professionals carried out their work profoundly affected agencies that were structured towards more conventional forms of service delivery (Darby and Williamson, 1978). This sense of chaos and the obvious inadequacy of existing services meant that, for those who suffered as a result of such violence, at best they could expect only haphazard response to their situation.

Direct rule and integrated service

We have described in Chapter 1 how the devolved government which had been in existence for 50 years in Northern Ireland, was eventually replaced by Direct Rule from London, in 1972. Although there are many factors which might help us understand the subsequent development of services during the Troubles, it can be argued that this change of political and administrative processes was very important. The shape and purpose of the newly constructed, integrated health and social welfare services which flowed from these political changes was quite profound (McCoy, 1993). When considered alongside the inability of the state to resolve the conflict, this organisational system was not best equipped to offer help to those who had been traumatised by violence in the decades that followed Bloody Sunday.

There are competing views on how beneficial this policy was. The way in which the integrated service was organised and delivered can be viewed either as part of a wider attempt to resolve long-standing problems of discrimination and sectarianism in the absence of social and political consensus between the 'two communities', or as a method of containing and managing a conflict in which the state had a part to play. It has been argued, for example, that the widespread use of quasi-autonomous governmental and non-governmental agencies in Northern Ireland during the period of Direct Rule was part of a rational strategy to remove power from a discredited local political system and place it the hands of a small group of ministers, their civil servants and non-discriminatory professionals (Birrell and Murie, 1980). A more critical appraisal of the rationale for Direct Rule suggests that central government used these mechanisms to at best manage, rather than resolve, the conflict (O'Dowd, Rolston and Tomlinson, 1980). Although there may have been some benefits in terms of conventional service delivery (Campbell and McLaughlin, 2000) the integrated service, however, was less effective in addressing the needs of people traumatised by violence. Campbell and Pinkerton (1997) and Pinkerton and Campbell (2002) have challenged the underlying assumption that staff could in fact make professional judgments somehow detached from experiences of living in such a conflictual society.

One of the consequences of the government's project, which often distanced state welfare bureaucracies from local communities, was that professionals and agencies were often unsure of how and when to intervene when traumatic incidents occurred. This critique of the state can be helpful in explaining why most health and social care professionals during these years were trained to deal with apolitical issues relatively efficiently, but tended to be poorly equipped to deal with their own, as well as, their clients' feelings about past and present violence. For example the effect of sectarianism helped to enforce a collective silence about potentially dangerous political and social agendas and prevent opportunities for reconciliation in the field of social work in Northern Ireland (Smyth and Campbell, 1996; Traynor, 1998; Campbell and Healey, 1999). At least social workers have made some attempts to address this issue in recent years (CCETSW, 1999); other professional groups such as doctors and nurses have barely acknowledged the impact of the conflict on their practice or have rarely had the opportunity to speak about how the violence has affected them (Smyth, Morrissey and Hamilton, 2001). The consequence of these sets of circumstances is that health and social care professionals have tended to attach great importance to 'normal' ways of functioning in this abnormal social and political context, a strategy which may be viewed as a way of distancing themselves from painful stories that clients sometimes disclose.

In the years that followed Bloody Sunday, policy makers and practitioners were generally unsuccessful in dealing with the traumas created by the Troubles. In fact, the first concerted attempt to deliver a comprehensive service in this area followed a civil incident. This was initiated as a result of the crash of an airplane carrying people from London to Belfast, nearly two decades after Bloody Sunday (Gibson, 1996), rather than any of the earlier Troubles-related incidents of the previous decades.

During the period of Direct Rule, the failure of politics and security policies (as discussed in Chapter 2) reinforced the perception of a society in stasis, with little opportunity for dialogue and conflict resolution. It is also interesting to note that, even where trauma-related services were delivered, this did not necessarily happen in a rationally organised fashion. The effect of much policy and practice was to render some groups apparently less deserving of services than others; the construction of a range of victimologies took place. For example members of paramilitaries and their families, many of whom were very unlikely to seek help from the state, gradually organised informal mechanisms of support for themselves and their communities. The growth in prisoner and ex-prisoner support groups over the years reflects this phenomenon (Crawford, 2003). On the other hand, security service members and their families tended to fall back on discreet forms of health and social welfare services, located outside, or hidden within, mainstream organisations, often for reasons of personal safety. Although there were a number of exceptions which illustrated good practice (Bolton, 1996), for the great majority of the population, trauma-based services were at best ad hoc and uneven. Many of these people were entirely innocent, what Bloomfield (NIO, 1998b: 30) described as the many 'little people' caught up in violence, often in relatively isolated incidents too soon forgotten outside the immediate family. Groups like the Bloody Sunday families were, in any case, unlikely to accept services because of their inherent distrust of the state. The unfortunate conclusion which can be drawn from this period was that the needs of the families were largely left unaddressed in much the same way that, 'for the remainder of the 1970s and 1980s the calls for justice from the relatives of Bloody Sunday victims fell largely on deaf ears' (Walsh, 2000: 287).

The ceasefires and after

It is only now, over a decade after the first Loyalist and Republican paramilitary ceasefires took place (1994) that policies and services for victims of the Troubles are being developed in a more comprehensive fashion. During this time a number of significant events, finally leading to the establishment of the Northern Ireland Assembly and an Executive led by local politicians, have allowed for some reflection on past violence and to consider new ways of dealing with trauma (McGarry, 2001; Morrissey and Smyth, 2002). Growing interest in researching the effects of the Troubles may lead to the conclusion that it is only in forthcoming years, using space created by a period of conflict resolution, that a well of previously unmet emotional and psychological need will be acknowledged and dealt with. It was during this period that groups such as the Bloody Sunday families became increasingly motivated to campaign for their rights as 'victims' or 'survivors', and to pursue justice for their relatives.

One event in the recent past has understandably become the focus of much attention in terms of policy in this area. On 28 August 1998 a bomb planted by the Real IRA (a group splintered from the Provisional IRA), in the town of Omagh killed 28 people and two unborn children. Another person was to die later. As the largest number of deaths created by any violent incident in the previous years of the Troubles in Northern Ireland, the Omagh bombing left an indelible impression on local, national and international opinion, coming as it did in the midst of the peace process and following the political settlement described in the Belfast Agreement (NIO, 1998a). The response of services at the time, in the aftermath of such a major traumatic incident, also suggested that workers were better equipped and more prepared for the consequent multi-layered problems faced by families and the community than they might have been in the past. This is not to say, however, that problems still remain for professionals in addressing their own painful emotions and memories of the past (Kapur, 2002; Reilly, 2000). In addition, the subsequent funding for a trauma centre, which was set up to deal with the sequelae of the Omagh bombing, has brought to light the problems of making difficult choices about the competing needs of other groups and geographical locations in Northern Ireland. (Morrissey and Smyth, 2002: 14–15).

In some ways such problems were at least recognised and beginning to be considered immediately before and after Omagh. On the first page of the Good Friday Agreement there is an explicit acknowledgement of the need to reorganise services and to find ways of dealing with the legacy of the past. Two reports (DHSS(NI), 1998; NIO, 1998b) in that year recognised the limitations of past services provided to those who have suffered. These reports recommend that:

- There should be recognition of all individuals and groups who have suffered.
- Welfare and legal services should be sensitive to the needs of those who have suffered.

- The voluntary and community sectors should be better supported.
- Statutory agencies should organise a comprehensive system of crisis teams.
- Professional psychology and counselling services should be expanded and accredited.
- Consideration should be given to a form of permanent memorial to victims.
- Adequate systems of compensation should be examined and arranged.

In the last few years the Northern Ireland Office, the Office of the First and Deputy First Minister, other departments at Stormont and a range of statutory and voluntary agencies, have established a number of projects to deal with victims' needs. Some of these developments are important in the context of the needs of Bloody Sunday families. What is apparent from these new policy initiatives is that there are high levels of unmet need amongst many individuals, groups and communities, and intense debate about how services should be constructed and delivered. One dilemma, for example, is the realisation that at one level there is a sense that some people have 'objectively' suffered more than others during the Troubles, in terms of physical, psychological, social and economic tragedy (Hamber, 1998), and yet it is difficult at the same time to measure one person's grief against another's. As an acknowledgment of the problems of achieving a universal definition, and perhaps to avoid rhetorical battles about victimhood, the government adopted the following definition: 'The surviving physically and psychologically injured of violent, conflict related incidents and those close relatives or partners who care for them, along with those close relatives or partners who mourn their dead' (OFDFM, 2002a: 1).

The report, *Reshape, Rebuild, Achieve* (OFDFM, 2002b) identifies a wide range of policies and strategies to address the needs of people who were traumatised, including:

- the improvement of service delivery
- ensuring cross-departmental responsiveness
- encouraging inter-organisational working

- establishing a variety of funding mechanisms to meet the diverse needs of victims and victims' groups.

The report, in listing the growing range of organisations involved in helping in Troubles-related fields, highlights a greater role for the voluntary and community sectors in this form of provision. The Department of Health, Social Services and Public Safety has also published a report on a review of counselling in Northern Ireland, part of which seeks to improve practice, education and training for those professionals who may be dealing with the needs of victims (DHSSPS, 2002).

The last few years has witnessed a significant increase in activity across a wide range of areas in response to these governmental reports and consultation with individuals, groups and the wider public (OFDFM, 2003). The government has set up an interdepartmental working group to respond to the apparent lack of coordination across sections of government. However, victims and survivors' groups continue to complain about the confusion caused by the split responsibility for this area between the NIO and OFDFM. Other developments include the creation of four Trauma Advisory Panels covering each health and social services board area in Northern Ireland, each with a full time coordinator to work with and develop services for victims/ survivors of the Troubles.

In the crucial area of funding, the Office has identified funds from the EU Programme for Peace and Reconciliation (Peace II) and has made available monies from a Victims' Programme Fund (2002–04) which is additional to a core funding scheme organised by the Northern Ireland Office. Another resource is the Strategy Implementation Fund to be accessed by government departments and agencies to fund projects and service for victims.

Although it is difficult to calculate an exact sum of this state expenditure, it has run into the tens of millions of pounds over the period since the signing of the Belfast Agreement. There have been some problems in both finding ways of distributing such resources equitably, and monitoring their use, particularly since there tend to be differences of perceptions about the purpose of such funding between government bodies and victims' groups. A significant, on-going tension continues to exist between the role of statutory bodies in providing services and developing community and voluntary sectors which are increasingly viewed by policy makers as an appropriate site for much of this activity (Clio, 2002). In addition, victims and survivors' groups find difficulties in submitting bids for funding due to the complexity of administration and paperwork. Furthermore, one of the most common complaints made about such schemes is the fact that, proportionately, funds for victims and survivors amount to only a tiny percentage of the overall Northern Irish government budget. It is hard not to conclude that this is only the start of a very long process which will take many years and considerably more funding to begin to address such high levels of unmet need.

Dealing with the trauma of the past

Although there is a perception that, at last, services to people who have been traumatised are improving, these alone may not be sufficient to meet hopes for justice and the resolution of trauma. The question remains as to whether Northern Irish society is currently willing or prepared to find some common ground to resolve the complex issues of blame, guilt and reparation which flow from the many traumatic incidents which have occurred during the Troubles (Morrissey and Smyth, 2002; Reilly, 2000). As in other areas of intense social and political violence around the world (Hamber, 1998; Hamber, 2000) the process of conflict resolution in Northern Ireland appears to have a long way to go before a sense of common trust emerges to allow such complex issues to be dealt with. The need to reflect upon past experiences should be viewed in parallel or complementary to psychological, health and social care service delivery.

The government's recognition of the *Healing through Remembering* Project which collated 108 submissions about how the process of remembering 'may address the legacy of the conflict in and about Northern Ireland' (OFDFM, 2002c: ii). As a result of this consultation process, six detailed recommendations were made:

- to develop networks of storytelling
- to build an archive of narratives or testimonies about the conflict

- to establish an annual day of reflection
- to construct a living memorial museum
- to find ways of encouraging all those involved in the conflict to acknowledge their responsibilities for political violence
- the examination of the possibility of creating a unique truth recovery process.

These proposals focus on the need to acknowledge individual and collective responsibilities for the past as a way of leading to expressions of truth and justice. These are crucial factors in the resolution of the types of trauma that have been experienced in Northern Ireland.

Helping the Bloody Sunday families

What then can this history and the policy and practice agendas of recent years tell us about the experiences of members of the Bloody Sunday families who have suffered so much in the last 30 years? In the early part of the Troubles, for some groups, such as the Bloody Sunday families, there was neither little prospect of being able to access services to meet their needs, nor opportunities to remember and process the traumatic events of the day and following years. On the contrary, from the moment of the trauma there is quite a lot of evidence from interview transcripts described previously in this book and other sources (Pringle and Jacobson, 2000: 285–95) to suggest that the action of authorities caused further pain and retraumatisation.

In the days and weeks that followed, family members suffered from acts of violence and intimidation after the march, travelling to and seeking help at Altnagelvin hospital, and in subsequent raids and harassment by security force personnel. It was possibly the case that health and social care professionals, however stretched their workload, might have been available to help families, but in the aftermath of Bloody Sunday, a lack of trust in these services was apparent. These themes were confirmed in interviews with some family members, during the original study conducted at the time of the 25th anniversary. Respondents were critical of the lack of social and health services available to them at the time of the trauma. As one family member said, 'People relied on neighbours and family to sort things out.' There was 'no counselling, only our faith in God'. Family members also acknowledged that they would not have accepted state supported social services at the time, not least because of the stigma they felt would have been attached to receiving such services. As one respondent put it, 'They would think we were crazy and would send us to Gransha' [the local psychiatric hospital]. Another viewed the relationship in a more sinister way: 'Even if help was offered, anyone employed by the establishment equals government, equals army, equals police.'

In such a politically charged situation that followed Bloody Sunday, it was likely that professionals and their agencies, who were barely equipped to deal with the events of the previous three or four years, could transform their services to deal with the calamitous aftermath of such a profound local event. In 1998, 26 years after the incident, this distance between the perceptions of the families and state services was largely confirmed in a seminar that disseminated preliminary findings of the study conducted at the time of the 25th anniversary to a sample of family members and professionals in Derry (Hayes, 1998). Family members were then, and still are, worried about issues of disclosure and confidentiality because of the history of complaints about how security forces might use personal information.

Health and social care workers also acknowledged that help given to people traumatised by the Troubles in Derry had been piecemeal and slow. One worker stated that no trauma services were available in 1972. If they had been 'they would have been offered, but (at the time) we didn't know anything about PTSD'. Even by the late 1990s there were no specific outreach services available to those affected by Bloody Sunday. One worker, fearing secondary traumatisation, said that she did not ask questions of her clients about the Troubles because she might uncover incredible pain that she feared she would 'take home with her'. She was also concerned because any work she would become engaged in would suffer because of a lack of adequate professional and managerial support. Another worker present at the workshop said they were told by supervisors during the Troubles to stay within their area of expertise and avoid other issues, because 'when you did stray, supervisors would say "don't touch it" and, to pursue it as a health professional, would make it seem too political'. One nurse at the meeting, who acknowledged the need to assist traumatised people, was reluctant to do so because she did not feel qualified and felt she might do more harm than good.

As we pointed out earlier in this chapter, it remains to be seen whether such initiatives are effective in addressing the issues which cause stress. The healing process for the survivors of Bloody Sunday and other traumatised groups may only be possible if professionals can build services in which citizens can participate and feel safe. In addition it is important that other, less tangible, but nonetheless, important mechanisms can be found which can help victims, and the wider society, come to terms with the trauma of the past.

In 2001 follow-up interviews with a subsection of the original respondents were carried out as a way of checking how perceptions may have changed in the five years since the initial study. Of particular interest to the authors was the way Bloody Sunday family members thought of service provision and which interventions, if any, would help them. The data which emerged revealed a mixture of disappointment, but sometimes hope, about the resolution of trauma which flowed from the event. Their stories were not uniform and they reflect diverse views on past and current service delivery and hopes that other events, such as the Saville Inquiry (discussed in Chapters 9 and 10) might bring resolution and justice.

State services

Old suspicions about trusting state services still persisted in narratives although some ambiguities emerged in the responses. One Bloody Sunday family member felt unsure about using such services: 'some of the families didn't agree with taking money from the state because it's coming from the British Government'. However he saw some contradictions in holding on to this position: 'on the other hand, they're using other services', notably medical services and other benefits which the state provides. He wondered how to 'narrow it all down ... draw the line? Where do you say, I am not accepting anything from the state?' He believed that 'whatever it takes, if somebody needs a facility to help them get through the process, use it'. He thought it was acceptable for local organisations to take government funding as a way of helping victims. Respondents were asked if services were available, what would be useful to them at this time. One family member replied, 'Phew, I don't know, because every individual's feeling differently. Certainly there are family members who are receiving some form of counselling at the present time.' Perhaps, another family member speculated, 'if the inquiry [the Saville Inquiry] had set up independent counselling services, people might trust these more.' She thought it would also be good to receive money directly from the state, and after 30 years, 'people should have learnt something in regards to that'. Another respondent also did not access services because 'maybe for years I didn't realise that I needed the help'. Once family members started dealing with it, as she put it, 'starting to work through, through having to fight, the inquiry and stuff', it made her realise she could not manage all of this by herself, 'I had locked it away for so long'. She too had negative feelings about social services being a state agency, but now she felt she could accept well-funded state services if they provided interventions which she could feel comfortable with.

For one man, the issue was not so much a criticism of state services, but that he had little faith that anyone could help him, given the degree of his mental ill health. This Bloody Sunday family member, who suffered symptoms of posttraumatic stress, had sought help from a psychiatrist at the local health centre, but thought that symptoms had been either minimised, not believed, or misunderstood:

> I went to the psychiatrist and the psychiatrist is telling me there's nothing wrong with me, 'You're quite sane.' Then as far as I am concerned, the rest of the world must be 'nuts' then, because if I'm sane at this particular moment everybody else is crazy. And that psychiatrist, I've no faith in them to be honest with you. I don't believe that there is anybody in Derry who would have the capabilities to properly counsel people like myself.

Another family member was also critical about psychiatrists

whom she believed could not fully understand the context of her suffering:

> Personally my own doctor is more help to me than the psychiatrist is, because I feel more comfortable with him. The psychiatrist not coming from Derry, she seems to be shocked about some things that I tell her. You know when I go there, she asks, 'How are you feeling today?' and I remember one time I said 'living in Creggan was hard' especially when there was house raids happening. There was occasions where there was a soldier left in people's attics and she looked at me in disbelief as if I was lying. She says 'Did that really happen?' I wondered then, 'Does she even live in the same country as me?'

This sort of experience convinced her that 'you need services from within your own community'. She felt she suffered from symptoms of Posttraumatic Stress Disorder, but that she was not getting the care or information she needed. She would like to know more:

> The only thing happens is every three to six months I would go down there and they ask, 'How are you?' I'm sure they know how to deal with people that has Posttraumatic Stress Disorder, but I haven't been offered anything. I'm sure the right way isn't to say, 'How are you?' and listen to you and say, 'I'll see you in three to six months time.'

She went on to question this type of service:

> Is there more to it than that or is this the way you are going to live the rest of your life? Can you wake up some day and say, 'I was ill and I'm no longer ill any more.' I want to know, is it treatable? Is there anything more that they can do other than give me antidepressants and change them and give me more and change them and give me more and ask me how I am?

Other respondents continued to feel that they were somehow different, not considered as victims like other people who have suffered other traumas in Northern Ireland. One expressed these feelings in the following way:

> No one has ever come forward to comfort relatives, over all the years, it has never happened. I'm talking about the official establishment if you want to call it, the DHSS [Department of Health and Social Services] and stuff like that there. When you look at the Omagh bombing and you look at the Enniskillen bombing, and you look at the others there, they were offered counselling straight away. Still 30 years on, counselling has never been offered to the families of Bloody Sunday. We went to the doctor. Counselling, you know, the doctor would certainly prescribe it, but it has never been voluntarily offered to the families and the victims, and the greater Derry community. It wasn't just the families and the people who were injured from it, there was a lot of people out there badly affected by Bloody Sunday emotionally, traumatically, every way whatsoever, and they are still carrying it 30 years on.

Another family member observed that some people who were victims of the Omagh bombing readily accepted state services, so there has been progress. Some respondents, however, appeared to have given up hope in finding help from formal organisations and professionals. One had rejected counselling and, instead, chose to cope by talking with friends who are likeminded in their views about the issues confronting them:

> If I've got a problem, I'll talk it over with him and if he has got a problem, he'll drop down here and we'll talk away basically amongst ourselves. If he's going through a bad time, I'll do what I can for him and he does the same for me.

He did finally tell his own physician about his symptoms and he received an antidepressant. He generally copes with depression, however, by drinking:

I'm saying prior to the inquiry [Saville Inquiry] I got drunk one day in the week, now with the inquiry on, maybe four, sometimes five. So yes, it's a depression. How do you deal with depression? I get drunk, I go out and get pissed out of my mind. For a couple of hours I can just basically forget all about it because I'm out.

Another family member said he probably wouldn't use services of any kind: 'I don't think I would be strong enough to deal, to go. I think it would be too sore on me.' He coped by keeping to himself, comes home, and the rest of the family all do the same. As he put it, 'You sort of feel more secure in your own environment.' One man explained that he had not availed of state services because he did not see how they could help him: 'We got nothin' and I don't expect anything, nor do I want anything of them. It's a bit late and maybe, if I had been offered it 10 or 15 years ago.' He finds self-help groups, friends and relatives to be helpful. He also goes out at times and has 'a good "jar"' [drink] and curses 'the world and all its woes and that's a bit of therapy. People might think it's stupid but you know, it works, you come home feeling a bit refreshed and relaxed.' The thing he says he needs from the state is not counselling, but recognition that his brother was murdered, that it was not his fault, that he was not doing something bad, that the family members are not evil people. He also wants his brother's death certificate corrected, which he has not been able to do:

That's the way they have treated us and I've never had any communication to my recollection from anybody in the social services, within government bodies to ask me or my family, 'How are you doing?' Far from it, we suffered after Bloody Sunday, harassment from the British security services.

Some respondents, however, recognised the need to be involved with and use state services 'when the time comes' but if and when that happened, they would want to have a part in the design of forms of service delivery.

Non-governmental agencies

In recent years a number of organisations have been funded to deal with the trauma of the Troubles in the Derry area. In addition, a few agencies deal specifically with the needs of the families of those who died on Bloody Sunday. In 1992, 20 years after the event some family members and other interested parties formed a pressure group, the Bloody Sunday Justice Campaign to highlight the injustice and develop systems of care and help. Following this initiative the Bloody Sunday Trust was established in 1997, 'with the aim of exploring the recent troubled history of the city of Derry as a sign of enhancing respect and understanding for human rights and promoting mutual understanding through the honest examination of the past' (www.bloodysundaytrust.org). At the same time a counselling service Cúnamh, was created 'to cater for the emotional and psychological impact which the conflict has had upon peoples' health and well-being' (www.cunamh.org). This organisation has been heavily involved in providing counselling and support services for families who attended the Saville Inquiry (discussed in Chapters 9 and 10). When they were interviewed, many respondents felt that these types of services should best be provided by local community groups, headed by trained leaders from their own cultural background, but supported by state funding. The fact that such groups are largely state funded (either directly or indirectly) perhaps indicates that, 30 years on, political processes have evolved sufficiently to lower earlier feelings of mistrust. It may be that community-based self-help groups, such as Cúnamh, will become the more acceptable mechanism for the funding and delivery of such services, somewhat detached from the state. As one family member put it, they 'should be given resources even if it appears to be duplicating existing services because, even if services are available they are not available'.

Some family members offered a range of both positive and negative comments about these local community-based services. A number thought Cúnamh to be 'pretty much too political', and criticised its involvement with a range of diverse causes, when it should be more focused on specific Bloody Sunday family needs. Others believed that the Bloody Sunday Trust which was set up to educate the public about the events of Bloody Sunday should have family members in control of the process. The implication was that family members' views were being unfairly subsumed in politicised agendas. As one respondent put it:

> I feel there's a sort of claiming exercise on in the name of Bloody Sunday. It's popular. To a point that some people are even suggesting this concerns the whole of Derry now and everything else. It does concern the whole of Derry but the point being there's a number of people who wanted to do something about Bloody Sunday because they lost somebody on Bloody Sunday, and because there was a loss of life on Bloody Sunday, that's why we have an inquiry. If there was no innocent lives lost on Bloody Sunday there would never be an inquiry.

In spite of the political divisions and mixed feelings about the mission and practices of Cúnamh, the organisation is recognised by some as being helpful to families, for example in supporting witnesses who are giving testimony at the Saville Inquiry. Another person said that the Bloody Sunday Centre family liaison officer also 'recognised the fact that people are badly affected by their giving evidence before the tribunal. There's always someone to assure that they're OK when they come out and so Cúnamh and the counsellor is vitally important in this process, vitally important.' However one family member had concerns about the professionalism of some of the work of Cúnamh, it was 'sort of part-time voluntary, right-hearted to start off with and then they started to engage workers because they got grants and everything else'. He said, however, that if he needed counselling:

> We have a national health service here and that's what should be done through your family doctor, appointed to a proper psychologist, well established, somebody who is capable of dealing with it. I have seen some of their counsellors from time to time and they were a bigger problem than state social services because they aren't trained to the standards they should be. The right heart and the wrong procedure doesn't help much.

He also believed that the many groups involved in Bloody Sunday may be 'polishing their own images and making quotas', not really serving families of victims, and that some people and organisations may be self-serving. Bloody Sunday has been his life for 30 years since he was 18 with most of that time 'spent in some form or faction dealing with Bloody Sunday'. The recent years have been particularly difficult because of his intense commitment to the Bloody Sunday Justice Campaign. As he put it, 'It really has had its toll even with my wife' – it is his wife who sat with him 14 hours a day doing research and she is the one who comforts him when he has nightmares. He relied on his wife, who was 'very strong' and is helping him to 'work and fight as hard as he can to find a proper conclusion for injustice of Bloody Sunday'. He did not want to be considered a victim and he felt that some groups with unqualified counsellors are promoting victimhood:

> I don't want to be a victim. I fight against that all the time. ... I think that a lot of these counselling groups especially if there are not properly set up, there's a danger in it. They create victims rather than resolving and trying to get the person to accept or to work through and come out at the other end healed and whole. You will never be totally healed and whole, but you can deal with it and move on. I find that a lot of them have created people who are victims and are always going to be victims and must see themselves as victims. Their life becomes being victims and they can't live without that. It's a false security but there is a certain security to it.

Another family member had never asked for state help but she valued the service from Cúnamh:

> They are good listeners. You need someone who is a good listener. I done a session there for eight weeks. You're throwing a lot into it. I was throwing out emotions that I didn't realise that I had.

Another man would use services now if they were available. He intended to go to Cúnamh last year but he 'just couldn't bring myself round to it'. He realised that he 'couldn't leave it any longer' especially with the testimony that was going to be given about his brother's death: 'I was afraid of something happening to me in the Guildhall. I wanted to be in as good a state as possible to receive information that was going to come out.'

Summary

This chapter described the history and development of state and community services for people who have suffered because of the Troubles. Until recently many of these services were neither equipped nor adequately funded to meet such complex needs, nor was the state a neutral player in these processes. Health and social care services during the two decades after Bloody Sunday were shaped by technocratic practice ideologies and a failure of politics to resolve the conflict. The emerging peace process during the last decade may provide opportunities to help and support those who have suffered, as well as finding ways of remembering and resolving the trauma of the past and present. Interestingly the family narratives collected and used in this book broadly reflect this changing set of circumstances, from an early, quite profound distrust of state services, towards a more positive vision of which types of services would be helpful.

Despite these developments there appear to be many unresolved emotional issues to be dealt with which are related to a sense of injustice about how the state has treated family members. These issues are discussed in more detail in the following chapters.

8 Bloody Sunday 30 years later

Patrick Hayes visited members of the Bloody Sunday families periodically during the years after his original interviews with them. During these visits he validated with them his interpretations of the stories they had told him at the time of the 25th anniversary. As the 30th anniversary approached, he explored their reactions to two major events in Northern Ireland over recent years: the peace process and the new inquiry into the events of Bloody Sunday. He followed the progress and outcomes of family storytelling since the 25th anniversary. The five tumultuous years from 1997 to 2002, as the inquiry process unfolded, were a time of great political change. In this chapter, we explore the traumatising and healing aspects of those events and the feelings of Bloody Sunday family members as they faced their fears and expressed their hopes for the inquiry and for peace in Northern Ireland. They continued their incomplete grieving process for their relative killed on Bloody Sunday and their ongoing quest for accessible, acceptable social and mental health services. They were ambivalent about the role of the media and its impact on events unfolding in Derry since the announcement of the inquiry and later, during daily proceedings. They were gratified to have the support of the Derry community as the inquiry process unfolded, yet sometimes annoyed with the public's expectations for them and intrusions into their private lives.

Experiencing the peace in Northern Ireland

The five years since the 25th anniversary were a time to deal not only with the prospect of the new inquiry, but also with adapting to and appreciating the peace in Northern Ireland. People were pleased that 'things are better, that the army is not on the street', that 'things are starting to mellow around', but they remained 'wary', and worried that 'it's going to break down'. Shattered trust, common in PTSD, was prevalent. As one family member remarked, 'There's no such thing as complete peace. You still be wary that some ugly animal is going to rear its head.' Another woman said scornfully, 'Well, I have seen nothing that has reassured me that I live in a safer environment and that my children should remain in Ireland.' She commented ruefully that the army and helicopters are still a presence and punishment beatings still happen, which served to remind her that her brother was 'murdered' and her father was injured. She contended that there has been no change for her, 'maybe for the North of Ireland as a whole', maybe for people who had not been affected by the Troubles. She failed to see 'any evidence of peace'. Living in a violent environment for over 30 years has made it difficult for some family members to adjust to the notion that suddenly, there is peace. Some 'can't be bothered' thinking about the peace process, and some think it 'a sham'. They blamed the Unionists for obstructing the process because 'they're not willing to accept wee bits and pieces, they want a complete capitulation'.

Frustration with problems in the political aspects of the peace process was apparent, however, family members hope that their lives will get back on track, that politicians will stop 'messing' with their future. They do not want to 'go back down that road again ... the last 30 years' because it would 'drive everybody into the mental hospital. It's wild hard to readjust again, but we got that taste of peace. I want that peace for my family.'

Derry, August 2001

The participants in this follow-up phase represented ten families. Ten participants of the original sample of 26 adults were available for interview. One earlier participant had died the previous year, two had had life threatening illnesses over the past five years. Several participants, very active members of the Bloody Sunday Justice campaign, did not remember specifics of their interviews five years earlier. They claimed that the interview was no different from others in which they had participated and it was not upsetting. It was a useful means to them for clearing their dead relative's name, and 'maybe raise the fact that he was murdered'. In stark contrast, several participants felt a strong impact from the interview. It had been like experiencing a flashback, which was frightening, but it marked the beginning of a healing process in which suppressed thoughts and memories about Bloody Sunday became words:

It is sometimes on your mind. You thought it wasn't. You didn't realise it was there. When people come to interview you, you go through all the emotions ... It's like a movie. The pictures all come back and they keep coming back, say for a day or week after you do an interview. It sort of drains you. After you left, it was a wee bit scary. I kept reliving that feeling, but then, I think I can talk better now. Funny, before it was too upsetting. It's not as bad as it was.

For others, that interview and those that followed helped to release long 'bottled up' tensions, helped to 'open things' that they had tried to forget, and helped them to come to terms with the events of Bloody Sunday. They were actually glad the interview had happened. For several participants, the interview was an organising experience in what had previously been a very chaotic emotional state, and they were now able to make sense of decades-long symptoms such as phobias, anxiety attacks, and depression. It also provided an opportunity to learn about Posttraumatic Stress Disorder and it gave them some relief:

It was the first time that I ever discussed Bloody Sunday in that kind of detail with anybody and it helped me to open up more. When the next person came along, then it did become easier. I find now that I am very open about it. I don't feel uncomfortable anymore talking about Bloody Sunday and the aftermath.

Several participants had never told their story about Bloody Sunday prior to the interview. It was not talked about in the family because it was too painful. They never thought anyone else would be interested in their story and how Bloody Sunday had affected them. In fact 'it was the first time that anyone had ever asked' how Bloody Sunday had affected them personally:

Every year on the anniversaries, on the news you would hear it. We didn't talk within the family about Bloody Sunday. So we had little or no information, and what little information we had, everybody seemed to be keeping it to themselves. So when you started doing the interviews, I think it was the first time that all the families really had that opportunity to speak.

It has always been difficult for some family members to talk about their experiences in the aftermath of Bloody Sunday. However, it was easier to talk with someone outside their families who could listen objectively. They felt free to unburden themselves and it helped, as a family member explained, 'because in the family you never find a really good time to talk about it, because it hurts. After all these years, it still hurts so much.' It also was fortuitous that Patrick Hayes was born in Derry and a stranger at first, but family members trusted that connection. Some remembered his mother and appreciated both his personal and professional interest, and that he had come such a long way to see them:

> You came across as a nice person and you made me feel very at ease. I could associate with somebody like yourself because you came so far a distance, and you were very into it. There were other people I wouldn't speak to at all. There were people who came from England.

After the 25th anniversary, one man acknowledged he 'had a wee touch of depression there for a while' because so many people were coming to Derry. He felt as though he was reliving everything with all the attendant emotion, but he is better now, 'able to handle it all right'. He added:

> Seeing you today down the town just brought back five years like a flash. Maybe that was a good thing that you came five years ago, because it sort of, it released emotion that I had for 25 years previous to that. When you came, it sort of eased out and then other people came and a wee bit more eased off.

His son who was not quite twelve at the time of the 25th anniversary remembered the interview very well. He found answers to many questions about Bloody Sunday and what had happened to his uncle. He admitted that he felt shocked the day of the interview, not only about the shooting of his uncle, but also because he 'found out that there were other people, and everything else that had happened that day. It was an even bigger shock again.' It was upsetting for him to see his father cry as he told his story. His father had never talked to him about what happened on Bloody Sunday until that day, but now both father and son can more easily engage in dialogue about those events.

Grieving the lost relative

Family members were asked if the Saville Inquiry has had any impact on their capacity to grieve the loss of their relative, which many had not been able to do. Circumstances surrounding the Widgery Tribunal and other issues in Northern Ireland contributed to a complicated bereavement for them. Family members' unresolved grief remained, and they were 'living it day in and day out'. They had cried at the time of the funerals, in 'their own form of grieving at the time of Bloody Sunday, when the bodies were in the house, when they were getting buried', but many family members believed that 'they've never had the opportunity to heal', due to what happened in the aftermath. They felt that the inquiry process is positive in helping them to 'open up' about their loss. For 20 years people remembered Bloody Sunday 'once a year' as 'something that happened a long time ago and 13 people had died', but as one man reported:

> Some months ago where something arose and my mother broke down, my sister broke down and my brother broke down, and I said to them, 'Wait a minute here, my mother's grieving after all these years. She's bottled it all up, let her cry.' I think that healing process may come once they're all proved innocent, maybe then. If he died in unfair circumstances, that it's at least being addressed now I suppose, but lots of things are dependent on the outcome.

Another family member's parents never discussed Bloody Sunday in their home, 'just put it in a suitcase, and put it under the bed. It was too much hurt. It was just locked away, was never brought out.' He hoped that the inquiry would help and he thought that 'this process is a good thing' for him. Another family member agreed, 'That's the reason why the inquiry was set up. If I didn't believe that then I wouldn't be there and if I haven't hope, then I have nothing.'

Janet (1920), Horowitz (1976), and van der Kolk (1994) argued that telling and retelling the story is a means of promoting trauma resolution and integrating the experiences into one's psyche. A family member confirmed that the process of listening to people telling the same story during the testimony at the inquiry, 'time after time, after time, after time' was validating. It helped her to cry, something she hasn't done 'a big lot other than maybe doing interviews or whatever'. It helped her 'to work through it, dealing with it on a daily basis. That's been a big help.'

At the time of Bloody Sunday many family members found no time for grieving. They were obliged to assume a parental role because their parents were disabled by the deaths of their sons. One man remembered crying, but that continued only for about 30 seconds to a minute because he 'had to take care of matters in the house' and then identify his brother's body at the morgue. He did not recall crying after that, but remembered feeling 'wild angry at the funerals' because of the way the funerals were handled and the presence of dignitaries. The funeral was taken away from family members since 'there wasn't room for them in the chapel and it was a nightmarish thing'. When his mother died two years later in a hospital in England, he had no time to grieve either. Again he was left in charge, with no time to cry because 'the Bogside at that time was crazy, and there was a shooting at the bottom of the street'. He was arrested taking one of the wounded to the hospital. Sometimes, 30 years later, he reported that sudden surges come upon him at the simplest thing said, and he stops it. Sometimes this happened when he was alone in the house. He described it as:

> A volcano inside you, but it only gets as far as the back of the eye and that's it and I hold that back. Sometimes I wish it would just rush out but it doesn't. It's held in check.

Another man also was unable to grieve because he simply could not remember the funerals. Just recently, with his immersion into the daily testimony at the Saville Inquiry, he could recall a terrifying repressed memory. He remembered 'quite clearly' being at the graveside and nearly falling into it as he lowered his brother's coffin:

> I was holding the rope on one side and was straddling one corner of the grave, and the crowd surged forward and as the crowd surged, I went forward and almost fell in. Now that was 29 years; it took me 29 years and it took a certain incident to bring that back to mind ... I think I've grieved it, but, in saying that, I can't remember crying, or anything like that.

There have been 'a lot of tears' since the beginning of the inquiry, but 'it's not tears of grief, it's tears of sadness' at what was seen there and what witnesses have said about their experience of what happened on Bloody Sunday. The grieving has not yet taken place, as the sister of a young man killed speculated: 'It won't take place until the inquiry ends and they come to whatever conclusion.' Another family member wanted to put Bloody Sunday behind him and in his remaining years have 'a bit of trust in society'. He agreed with other family members that the potential to put the grief to rest and to regain some trust depends largely on Judge Saville and what he finds, but, he expressed fearfully, 'If it's another Widgery ... the consequences it will have on the family!'

Living with the inquiry

Over the past five years the Saville Inquiry has had a most decided effect on family members' lives. When English Prime Minister Tony Blair commissioned a new inquiry into the events of Bloody Sunday, family members were extremely gratified. Mr. Blair's decision was the direct result of many years of persistent efforts by the Bloody Sunday Justice Campaign. Family members, however, probably did not anticipate fully the intensity and commitment needed to follow through with the process. The inquiry has dominated some family members' lives and they attend the sessions daily because they feel it is something they have worked for and, they hope, will help them find closure and peace. Others are afraid of 'being sucked in' and prefer to remain somewhat distant in their involvement:

I'm conscious of it and, I suppose to some extent, quite selfish. I mean I go when I can, but if I'm working, then I'm not there and I suppose even when I wasn't working. If I'm not working, I like to get in maybe once or twice a week but I'm not fanatical about being there and I'm really quite determined that it won't consume my life.

The inquiry has also forced family members to be more political, something they never wanted because they 'were family orientated straight down the middle', but they seemed to be 'dragged into politics, which was the last thing in the world' they wanted. The past five years have been a time of hard work, by 'ordinary lay people who took on the British establishment'. They knew nothing about the law but 'all of a sudden things started to build'. They were greatly excited with the announcement of the inquiry, frustrated at delays in the commencement of proceedings, and disappointed with postponements related to the magnitude of the task, the need to sift through evidence, and uncertainty as to what the outcomes would or should be:

> People talked about apologies, and apology was totally unacceptable to us because as someone said one time, 'you can apologise to the living; you can't apologise to the dead'. Plus the fact too at the end of the day, the truth about what happened on Bloody Sunday wouldn't have come out through an apology, so it was important that the issue itself was addressed, and addressed openly, and when we reached the inquiry we didn't even know what was going to happen then.

Disappointments centred around the selection of judges for the inquiry and issues related to anonymity for soldiers involved in the shootings. They were not happy that the chairman is English. Some family members were deeply involved in the inquiry and this affected their personal and mental health. The inquiry has been 'very difficult' for some people, and 'bouts of depression' are common. Going to the inquiry feels like a 'hard day's work'. As one family member said, 'I come in here mentally exhausted where I wouldn't be fit to even make a cup of tea for myself.' Sleep difficulties and intrusive thoughts were common, particularly after disturbing testimony:

> You don't sleep. What you do is you lay yourself out but you don't sleep. How can anybody possibly sleep after hearing that? It goes round in your mind and you trying to understand how somebody else could do that. It's something that I can't understand, the injustice behind it. How a human being can treat another human being like that. I couldn't treat an animal like that and to say that they were animals for doing that would be an insult to animals. They're worse than that, because I would treat an animal with respect.

Sleeplessness related to intrusive thoughts is typical of PTSD as is a compulsive need to organise these thoughts through journal writing. One man always woke during the night and obsessed about arguments he heard the previous day from a soldier's representative or one of the council. He tried to 'deal with that by writing it down on a bit of paper'. Listening to the evidence 'day in and day out' was wearing. Family members constantly thought about 'the stories of nearly up to five to six people per day' and this was 'very hard to live with'. Self-medicating with alcohol as a means of coping with intrusions was a problem for some:

> All the talk has actually affected my health possibly in a physical way and maybe to a certain extent in a mental way as well, because, you know, I take a drink. The drinking habit is now extended beyond one day a week and depending on how things would go during the inquiry, myself and a friend of mine could possibly end up in the pub nearly three days a week now to try and forget the events that we had to listen to that particular day.

As they struggled to cope with the stories being told during the inquiry, some family members felt pressured to be 'experts' about all aspects of the testimony being offered, obliged to answer 'a million questions'. It seemed as if they were always being asked, 'What are you going to do about this?' as if the family members bore sole responsibility for the outcomes. Community members often made suggestions such as, 'You have got to fight this, you know' particularly the issues related to excusing soldiers from 'giving their evidence at the inquiry'. They seldom experienced respite even if they left town on holiday:

> So it's really, really stressful, and even the one week we had which was in Donegal, I was still approached by people and they wanted to know all about the inquiry, what was happening, who was up giving evidence, what their stories were. People were forever asking what was going to happen in relation to the soldiers.

One family member tried to relax after the end of the week of attendance at the inquiry, but she could not escape, she complained, 'because no matter where you go, all people wanted to talk about was the inquiry, so as to be a wee bit diplomatic', her response to them was, 'I don't like talking about it when I have a drink in me.' What she really wanted to say was, 'Fuck away off! I don't want to talk about it tonight.'

Another family member was genuinely glad to talk to people about what was happening in the inquiry, and he wanted to assure others that they were getting accurate information. He was grateful for their support, but when he tried to be away from the inquiry, even in church or at the sports complex, people stopped him and offered either good wishes or opinions. He was ambivalent about being a conduit for information, a community identified representative for the families, and reluctant to deal with the tremendous stress that this imposed upon him. He found it exhausting to repeat the same story after being in the Guildhall for six or seven hours, and then feel obliged to speak with his solicitor afterwards. He thought he could escape by going home or to a pub, but family members and others wanted to talk with him about the events of the day at the inquiry. He finds this oppressive. While he would never end the process prematurely, there are times when he thinks:

> Oh don't, nobody ask me again please, 'cause I'm telling the same story and that's really very annoying, very tiring,

because I have a headache and I don't care. But I can't get
away from it. I just can't get away from it.

Additionally, several family members had the responsibility for
administrative functions related to the inquiry. This responsibility
was another source of stress with 'an awful lot of work still to be
done' creating and maintaining databases, particularly in prepara-
tion for the testimony of the soldiers involved in the shootings on
Bloody Sunday. They 'want to know and to search as much as they
can and have it on the database so it can easily be called up'. Two
family members experienced a life-threatening illness, but recovered; another admitted that the stress of the inquiry had caused
strain in his marriage. He explained, 'It tends to overflow into
other aspects of your life.' He confided that he would 'love to give
it up' because of all the pain and frustration. The frustration, he
stressed, is 'worse than anything else. Sometimes the lack of belief
in yourself that you're going to get the true result, leads to that
awful frustration that creates an anger within you and that isn't
good for your health and mentality.' He was diagnosed with
'about six different problems' and experienced 'bouts of depression'. He coped by going for walks, but when he was 'really down'
he revisited places his family went when he was a child. These
visits were a way of 'getting back in touch with a sense of belonging, a sense of reality or proportion, like a pilgrimage sort of
thing'. He acknowledged that others in his family also suffered
from depression, one for more than 20 years. His younger siblings
coped reasonably well because the 'quest for justice was something they have lived with for a very long time', perhaps something that they preferred not to address, but they would 'feel
guilty' if they did not continue.
   Another family member remarked that among her twelve
siblings, only one was 'positively healthy', and she attributed this
to the fact that she lived away from Northern Ireland. Family
health has deteriorated, and two siblings were advised by physicians that attendance at the inquiry was not in the best interest of
their health. The entire family was warned that the inquiry would
be traumatic, but, he professed, 'this is something that you feel
that you have to do, because we only know a part of Bloody
Sunday, but we want to know everything that happened'. Another

family member reported optimistically that her 'health has been quite good' except for her sleeping pattern, which she attributes to ageing or 'change of life'. As with others, her mind 'comes alive' in the middle of the night. While she attempts to dismiss this with a positive, light-hearted explanation, she may be denying that she is suffering from intrusions related to Bloody Sunday.

The media and Derry community response to the inquiry

Family members were asked how the inquiry process impacted their lives in the Derry community and how they perceived media coverage of daily events. Newspaper and television coverage brought Bloody Sunday issues 'big time into the public domain' and 'there's a lot of buzz', which made people in Derry very aware of what was happening. Derry residents had a vested interest in the outcomes of the inquiry, as one family member explained: 'The atrocity happened to them as much as it happened to me and my brother. It was just a lottery he was going to die, and he did die, and I'm very aware of that. I could have been going to somebody else's funeral instead of my brother's.'

Family members were generally sceptical about media reports of the inquiry. This distrust may have been founded in reality, but was likely compounded by the long ago trauma that has compromised their sense of trust. This scepticism put additional pressure on them to be guardians of truth and to be the ones to 'set the record straight'. Several family members commented that sometimes there were discrepancies between media reports and what actually happened at the inquiry and they argued, 'The media is there to sell newspapers and they can put "slights" on and shine things in certain ways' or give 'a distorted view of what was really said, and reporters are good at twisting the truth'. What was reported and what actually happened were 'two different things', so family members sometimes needed to 'explain things to people'.

Generally, however, 'the media is not bad', but they did 'have to grab a headline' after listening to hours of evidence, and as one family member insisted, 'there are times I've seen the story in the press that is totally false in regards to what has happened in the Guildhall. They take three or four sentences of this or that and they have compiled the story how they see is going to sell a news-paper.' He argued that people reached incorrect conclusions about what was happening as a consequence. This created a false confi-dence because people assumed all was well, but regarding certain matters, he exclaimed, 'in truth the value of the day was between 0 and 10 or only 1 or it might have been minus 1!

Another family member believed that the media sometimes glamorised events. He remained sceptical of their intentions and preferred not to talk with them. He could 'see the glamour and the news to sell newspapers', but he believed this sends out the wrong message. He explained, 'I don't like to see the thing glamorised because there is no glamour in it, no glamour in murder.'

Generally, as one family member reported, 'most of the media have been quite good to us, particularly from the onset of the inquiry'. She does admit she harboured a deep distrust and 'a fear of the media, having to talk to people, or do interviews, or anything like that'. She added that the *Daily Mirror* was now being printed in Derry and wondered if the version printed there was the same as that printed in England. During the inquiry, as at the time of Bloody Sunday, she explained, people believed what they were told, which vilified her brother and the other families' rela-tives. She continued, 'So, there's still that, and as the saying goes "if you throw enough muck, some of it is going to stick" and let's face it, a lot of it stuck'. She recounted an experience that validated her beliefs about the media tailoring the news for its audience. An English woman visited the inquiry and listened to the testimonies. She learned that things were different from what she had always believed and she was upset by the revelations:

> This lady came into the Bloody Sunday Centre. She looked as if she was upset, and my sister goes to her and says, 'Are you OK?' She started to cry and she says, 'I'm ashamed to be English.' My twin sister says to her, 'You have nothing to feel ashamed about. It was only a certain amount of people that was responsible, but you are not responsible.' So the feeling is starting to filter through.

In spite of mixed feelings about the media and its potential for distortion, many family members thought that news coverage created an atmosphere which allowed people to talk more freely about Bloody Sunday. Conversations were easier, a big change, an important element in resolving trauma. Derry people were 'open and more relaxed, not scared or afraid about saying the wrong thing'. Many people from the community have stepped forward to testify and afterwards, there is animated conversation among those who told their stories.

Some family members were cynical or pessimistic about the outcome. This is a source of irritation to other family members who felt that Derry people had a 'chance to deal with it ... could tell their stories' and were no longer ignored as they were at the Widgery Tribunal. In general, the inquiry into the events of Bloody Sunday was viewed positively, which allowed the people of Derry to begin 'to put it into its proper place and start to move on'. They felt that this resolution was so important, 'because there's a lot of alcoholism out there, not totally to do with Bloody Sunday, but a lot of it to do with Bloody Sunday because it was people's way of coping'.

The Derry community was always an 'extended family' to Bloody Sunday family members, who felt community support because 'people in the street every now and again say to them, 'You are doing a great job.' Complete strangers, they said gratefully, 'come up to you ... and they show themselves for what they are: friends. People are behind you.' If family members have a bad day in court, feedback from people validated their experience with empathic statements such as, 'That was terrible! What is that happening?'

Family members deeply appreciated community members' attendance at the inquiry and would like more to experience 'first hand' what happens on a daily basis. When people from Derry attended, family members felt that people were 'actually looking out' for them, 'keeping an eye on things'. They admired ordinary people who 'were incredibly brave in giving testimony'. It was 'brilliant the fact that they've come along, to be able to shed any light on what happened that day' to help 'solve the puzzle', even with what might seem to be the most insignificant piece of information. Family members also were aware that many Derry residents did not seem to understand the public nature of the inquiry, perhaps felt excluded or reluctant to attend, as if the inquiry were a private process. A family member explained, 'It's like if some-body's up in court, you don't dive in to see what's going on, and this seems to be the thinking on it.'

Summary

This chapter provided a background to reactions of Bloody Sunday Family members to events in Northern Ireland in the five years since the 25th anniversary. The peace process was important in the lives of family members, yet reactions were mixed, with significant doubt. The Saville Inquiry into the events of Bloody Sunday was the overriding issue and concern for most. The inquiry has been a factor in promoting discussion about Bloody Sunday in the media and among the residents of the Derry community. The community has been supportive of family members, with many willing to offer testimony about the events of Bloody Sunday. Sometimes, however, community members were intruding into the lives of family members, offering opinions and asking for updates, yet reluctant to attend the daily sessions so they could formulate their own conclusions. Reactions to media coverage include doubts about the accuracy of information reported during the daily conduct of testimony at the inquiry. Family members' hopes, fears and doubts about resolution of their trauma and capacity to finally grieve their dead are inexorably linked to the outcomes of the inquiry.

9 The quest for justice and resolution of trauma? The Saville Inquiry

A number of themes emerged from the new follow-up interviews described in other chapters in this book. In the preceding five years a number of momentous events occurred which may have had the effect of changing both state and public attitudes to Bloody Sunday. Before then many of the families had endured failed attempts to have their case heard either in court or at political levels. For years following the event it may be assumed that the feelings of trauma, suffering and sense of injustice remained unresolved. As some of the interviews in earlier chapters suggest, guilt by association and harassment must have compounded these emotions. Walsh (2000) describes these early years and the unsuccessful attempts by family members to have their voices heard. Opportunities to pursue criminal prosecutions were removed by the Director of Public Prosecutions in 1972, paltry ex gratia payments, which denied any liability by the state, were paid to family members, and an inquest in 1973 was hindered by the narrow rules of the Northern Irish legal procedures. By the early 1990s, however, the Bloody Sunday Justice Campaign and other groups were pushing to have the case re-examined. At the time of the 25th anniversary in 1997, a range of factors were creating pressure to have a new public inquiry established.

Mullan's book, *Eyewitness Bloody Sunday* (1997) used newly discovered Cabinet papers, over 100 eyewitness accounts which had been disregarded by the Widgery Tribunal, and other material to argue that the killings and injuries were unjust and that the British political and military establishments were complicit in the massacre. He raised the additional possibility that three of the people may have been killed by shots from the city walls and not by the Parachute Regiment which had operated on the ground in the Bogside. His publication, a subsequent Channel 4 news report, the discovery of 'Porter tapes' (amateur radio intercepts of army and police communications on the day) and the *Walsh Report* which critically analysed original statements by soldiers given to the Widgery Tribunal, led to political movement on the issue (Mullan, 1997: 301). A series of meetings then took place between families, activists and British and Irish governments, which eventually culminated in the announcement on 29 January 1998 by the British Prime Minister, Tony Blair, that a new inquiry would be established.

It has been argued that much of the root cause of the continued sense of injustice amongst family members, the Derry community and wider society over the last 30 years has been the way in which the original Widgery Tribunal (1972) was structured and carried out. The Tribunal has been heavily criticised because of the manner of its operation and the incoherence of conclusions that were drawn from limited facts (McCann, Shiels and Hannigan, 1992; Mullan, 1997; Walsh, 2000). The traumatic effect of the killings was probably compounded and magnified by the flawed and contentious nature of this Tribunal. From its very origins it is now apparent that the assumed separation between the political executive and judiciary was breached before, during and after proceedings.

Mullan (1997) and Walsh (2000) used cabinet minute papers uncovered by Ruth Winter, which record discussions between the then Prime Minister, Edward Heath, the Lord Chancellor, Lord Hailsham, and the Lord Chief Justice, Lord Widgery, to highlight the way in which the terms of reference for the Tribunal were unnecessarily limited. Not only was there a sense of undue expeditiousness, it is now clear that the Tribunal was, from the beginning, overtly political in its function. This was confirmed in the way in which Heath reminded Widgery that, 'we were in Northern Ireland fighting not only a military war, but a propaganda war' (Winter in Mullan, 1997: 27).

Arguably the most problematic aspect of the terms of reference for the Tribunal was the insistence by Widgery that it would focus only on the immediate events of the day, primarily during the time when the shootings took place. McCann, Shiels and Hannigan (1992) have shown how even this principle was occasionally broken by Widgery when he, from the start, allocated blame to those who organised the illegal march, and used accounts of violence, constructed by the British Army, which affected the Bogside in the months which preceded Bloody Sunday. In contrast, little attempt was made to examine strategic political and security force decision making before, during and after the event.

There were also internal inconsistencies in the function of the Tribunal. Little attempt was made to resolve conflicting evidence, to give evidence due and proper weight, forensic evidence was unreliable, an incorrect application of the law on legal force was used, and conclusions were not supported by facts (Winter in Mullan, 1997: 26). In addition, Widgery refused to accept, or take account of, around 700 eyewitness statements, many of which were collected soon after the event by the Northern Ireland Civil Rights Association (NICRA). Furthermore, the haste in which the Tribunal took place did not allow people who had been injured to testify.

Walsh has also pointed out many fundamental legal inconsistencies which characterised the Tribunal. Widgery himself was a former officer in the British Army, the secretariat were too close to the government, and even interfered with the drafting of the report. Families were provided with inadequate legal counsel and a decision was made on security grounds to hold the Tribunal in Coleraine, a Unionist town some considerable distance from Derry. Subsequent examination of army statements by Walsh has suggested that government lawyers may have 'coached' these witnesses, and that statements had been changed, sometimes on a number of occasions. Despite this statements often contradicted each other.

Given the inherent bias in the terms of reference and operation of the Tribunal, the growing concerns of the families and wider Derry community at the time of the hearings were confirmed in the report that followed. After only a few months the Tribunal completed its work and the report was published. The shortness and inadequacy of the document appears in inverse proportion to such a profound event in which so many lost their lives and were injured. There are moments when Widgery is critical of the action of some soldiers, for example in the case of soldier 'H' who could not account for 19 of the 23 rounds of ammunition he expended. Security force personnel remained somehow exonerated on the basis that they were under fire, although there is little concrete evidence to suggest that this was the case. On the other hand, a shadow of doubt of culpability was left with many of the victims, either directly or by implication.

Although the families of those killed, and people who were injured were eventually compensated by the government through ex gratia payments (Pringle and Jacobson, 2000: 295) legal responsibility has, to date, not been acknowledged. For many of the families and the wider community the apparent injustices of the Widgery Tribunal have simply compounded their sense of grief and trauma. Twenty-six years after the event the current Saville Inquiry began its work on 3 April 1998. Its terms of reference were outlined by the Prime Minister, Tony Blair:

> It is expedient that a Tribunal be established for inquiring into a definite matter of urgent public importance, namely the events on Sunday 30 January 1972 which led to loss of life in connection with the procession in Londonderry on that day, taking into account of any new information relevant to the events on that day.

The Inquiry structure and process

The Official Bloody Sunday website describes the Inquiry purpose and process (www.bloody-sunday-inquiry.org). The Inquiry was to establish the existence and examination of any new evidence that was not available to the Widgery Tribunal – the discovery of new evidence was probable given the limited timescale and remit of Widgery. The Inquiry was set up under the Tribunals of Inquiry (Evidence) Act 1921. This meant that the Inquiry had the same legal powers as the High Court to require individuals to attend before it and to provide documents. The Inquiry was conducted by an international tribunal of judges, chaired by Lord Saville of Newdigate. The other Inquiry members are William L. Hoyt (formerly Chief Justice of New Brunswick, Canada) and John L. Toohey (former Justice of the High Court of Australia, who replaced Sir Edward Somers who resigned for personal reasons in July 2000).

The Tribunal, Counsel, the Inquiry Solicitor and the Inquiry Secretary all had the same duty, which was to seek the truth about what happened on Bloody Sunday. That duty, which was the object of the Inquiry, was to be carried out using an inquisitorial rather than adversarial style in seeking the truth. The role of the Counsel to the Inquiry, Christopher Clarke QC, and his assistants was to advise the Inquiry and to assist it by presenting the evidence to the Inquiry and questioning the witnesses on their behalf. The opening statement from Lord Saville was made on 3 April 1999. Oral hearings commenced on 27 March 2000. The opening speech by Christopher Clarke lasted for 42 days of sittings over a three-month period – the longest in British legal history. The first witness to give oral evidence was heard on 28 November 2000 and the closing summation commenced on 4 October 2004. However evidence was heard from an additional witness in January 2005.

An important lacuna in Inquiry proceedings took place in 2003. The hearings moved from the Guildhall in Derry to Central Hall, Westminster, London between Tuesday 24 September 2002 and 21 October 2003. This was because the Court of Appeal ruled that soldier witnesses had reasonable fears for their safety. The Inquiry then returned to the Guildhall Derry on 29 October 2003 to hear the remaining oral evidence, which was completed on 13 February 2004. Written submissions were then delivered to the Inquiry and all other Interested Parties by 12 March 2004, written submissions in reply delivered to the Inquiry and all other Interested Parties by 23 April 2004 and an oral session was held at the Guildhall on 7 June 2004 which allowed the Inquiry to seek any necessary clarification of written submissions. The Inquiry sat for over 400 days and heard over 900 witnesses.

Legal procedures

Although this was an inquisitorial Inquiry, representation was offered to the families of those who died on Bloody Sunday, those who were wounded, and security force personnel. Normally, questions were put to witnesses by Counsel to the Inquiry. When appropriate, and subject to the discretion of the Inquiry members, questions were put by Counsel for the interested parties. The Inquiry also questioned some witnesses. In some instances witnesses (mostly members of the security forces) were 'screened' while giving their evidence. This meant they were only visible to the

Inquiry members, counsel and other legal representatives. Members of the public and media could hear the evidence being delivered but could not see the witness while this was done, although the witness's name was in the public domain unless application for anonymity was granted. The Inquiry ruled in October 1999 that every soldier whose identity was not already clearly in the public domain would not be identified in the course of the Inquiry's proceedings unless the Inquiry members directed or ruled otherwise. This gave effect to the judgement of the Court of Appeal in 28 July 1999. However, the Attorney General stipulated that any written material or oral evidence provided by a witness could not be used to incriminate that witness in any later criminal proceedings. It was considered essential that in order to reach the truth of what happened on Bloody Sunday witnesses did not refuse to cooperate on the grounds that they may incriminate themselves. This did not rule out the possibility of future criminal proceedings against an individual, only that their own evidence to the Bloody Sunday Inquiry could not be used against them.

The media and the public were encouraged to attend the hearings. In the Guildhall the upper gallery had 100 seats reserved for the public and the lower gallery had separate areas for the use of family members and the media. A media centre was also located nearby where land lines, a fax, ISDN line, photocopier and CCTV/document screens were available to journalists. The media centre could seat up to 20 people. The Inquiry website provided a list of witnesses, transcripts of proceedings and witness statements. Unless the Inquiry directed otherwise, all documents put in evidence were displayed on screens in the main hall and wherever there was CCTV coverage of the proceedings. This enabled the press and public to view the activities of the Inquiry.

The magnitude and cost of the Inquiry

The Inquiry interviewed and received statements from around 1,800 people with about half of these giving oral evidence. Of these, 504 were civilians, 245 military personnel, 49 media, 39 politicians or civil servants, 33 members of the RUC, 34 members or former members of paramilitary organisations, nine experts or forensic scientists and seven priests. A total of 35 bundles of evidence, each comprising approximately 150 volumes, including 12 volumes of photographs, were sent to representatives of the interested parties to the Inquiry. In addition 41 audiotapes and 62 videotapes were circulated. It has been estimated that the eventual total cost of the Inquiry to Government will be over £150 million.

Strengths and weaknesses of the Inquiry

Given the political and legal background to the Inquiry, its length of time in deliberation and substantial costs, it is not surprising that a range of competing views have emerged over the five years about its purpose and efficacy. An early critic of British government's handling of Bloody Sunday (Walsh, 2002) has described a number of positive aspects of the Inquiry, at its mid-point, which distinguished it from the Widgery Tribunal. The Inquiry was comprised of three judges, two of whom were from outside the jurisdiction of the United Kingdom. It may be assumed that this balance will have encouraged family members to believe in the objectivity and independence of the Inquiry, in contrast to the perceived partiality and bias of the Widgery Tribunal. Walsh argued that confidence in the Inquiry was probably strengthened by its willingness to engage in a thorough search for key witnesses and relevant evidence from a broad array of sources. The Inquiry was served by a counsel and independent solicitors, and widespread use was made of information technology. This perception of rigour was further reinforced by the Inquiry's threat to use the power of subpoena to access such information. Thus the Inquiry, at times, compelled some witnesses to attend to give evidence and required important material from journalists and security agencies to be presented. Arguably the work of the Inquiry was also enhanced by a decision to grant immunity from prosecution for witnesses in respect of evidence which they provided, although there it is probably the case that, conversely, many family members will have felt that prosecution of those who killed their relatives was an important process along the road to truth and justice. Walsh asserts that the Inquiry was largely successful in revealing a "substantial new body of evidence about Bloody Sunday" (Walsh, 2002: 2).

A number of criticisms, however, have been made about the Inquiry from a range of interest groups. These were revealed in the challenges to the proceedings in the High Court and Court of Appeal. Walsh described the first significant challenge raised by the lawyers representing the families of the deceased. The families were dissatisfied with the decision to restrict legal representation to one leading and two junior counsel. One of the reasons given for this decision was that by increasing levels of legal representation, the Inquiry might be turned into an adversarial rather than inquisitorial process. On reconsideration, perhaps because of the families' jaundiced experience of inadequate legal representation during the Widgery Tribunal, this decision was reversed. More extensive legal representation was granted to the families, although the financial costs to the public fund because of legal fees, both for the state and the families, were to become a bone of contention in the wider context of Northern Irish politics.

Walsh further described the next major issue of contention for the Inquiry – the question of witness anonymity. Although the hope of the Inquiry was that by granting anonymity more evidence would be forthcoming, this was a problematic condition for family members in particular, and the wider community in general. Many felt it was of fundamental importance that those who may have been involved in the killings and violence of the day should be present and recognisable in court, as part of the process of justice. For their part, members of the army, police and others felt they needed full anonymity on grounds of security and safety. Initially the Inquiry sought to limit anonymity to the publication of addresses and personal details. On appeal to the High Court, and then the Court of Appeal, decisions were made against the Inquiry's position on anonymity. It was argued at appeal that the Inquiry had placed too much emphasis on the need for procedural transparency at the expense of the rights of witnesses to be protected against possible harm which may have resulted if their anonymity had not been fully granted. The outcome was that the Inquiry was required to grant anonymity to security force personnel who applied for it, unless their name was already in the public domain. Walsh then described the way in which soldiers' legal representatives went on to challenge the requirement that they should give evidence in the Guildhall in Derry, because of fears for their safety. The Inquiry argued that the location of the Guildhall was important in the context of its mission to uncover the truth about what happened in Derry in 1972; it was appropriate that public hearings take place in the city. Once again, however, appeals to the High Court and Court of Appeal by the soldiers reversed the decision of the Inquiry. The Inquiry was therefore moved to London for the period when soldiers provided witness statements.

Walsh concluded his article by suggesting that a number of legal and procedural gains emerged as a result of the Inquiry and that these experiences led to substantial contributions to the law and practice of such tribunals in the United Kingdom. For example the High Court and Court of Appeal rulings on anonymity and the decision to move the venue established certain principles about the protection of witnesses and their rights in these situations. In addition he argued that there was intrinsic interest in some of the Inquiry's own rulings in the areas of:

> rights of representation, access to confidential security information and journalistic sources, as well as the basic nature and methodology of a tribunal of inquiry.
>
> (Walsh, 2002: 4)

Will the Inquiry establish the truth and heal the wounds?

Although the purpose of the Inquiry was to seek the truth about what happened on Bloody Sunday, as the years have gone by many parties within and outside Northern Ireland have questioned whether such an Inquiry could bring resolution to those who have been affected by the event. The complicated nature and processes involved in finding truth, reconciliation and trauma resolution has been examined in the context of other conflicts around the world (Hamber, 1998). The focus of interest in Northern Ireland has often been on the particular model used by the South African Truth and Reconciliation Commission (TRC) (Hamber, 2003). It would, however be wrong to draw explicit parallels between a public investigation such as the Saville Inquiry, designed to seek the 'truth' or 'facts' about a single, violent event, and the much broader terms of the most internationally quoted forum. The TRC, for example, examined many violent events over the period of Apartheid; South Africa is a society with quite diverse social, economic and political contexts and at another moment in the transformation of a different type of conflict. Importantly the Commission found it necessary to dispense with what might be described as conventional legal process by accepting the need to trade truth for formal justice by granting amnesties for those who told their story. Although the TRC was partially successful in helping build towards wider process of national reconciliation, the hopes for truth and justice carried by many of the over 20,000 people who participated, were not fulfilled. It has been argued that this has left substantial amounts of individual and group psychological and material needs unmet. The argument for a TRC for Northern Ireland will be tempered by such findings. An even greater complication is the relative absence of a consensus about the need to address past wrongs at this stage of the process of conflict resolution.

It is a moot point whether the outcome of the Saville Inquiry will affect the families' views on justice and closure; the Inquiry, unlike a truth commission has a much narrower focus. It sought to examine any new information, relevant to the events of the day, which has emerged since the publication of the Widgery Report. However, this term 'relevant to the events of the day' will touch upon many painful issues hitherto avoided, including the role of state security forces, paramilitaries, politicians and other parties before and after the event. For these reasons it would be foolish to assume that the outcome of the Inquiry can be a panacea for all the problems experienced by the families who lost relatives on Bloody Sunday. In any case, these individuals are not a homogenous group, and it would be wrong to generalise about this, and many other issues, for all the relatives. It is inevitable that families reflect a variety of social, political and moral standpoints that affect their views on the merits of the Saville Inquiry. As Morrissey and Smyth (2002: 188) point out, such public events may for some people cause further trauma through the reliving of painful memories they would prefer to forget, just as much as giving hope of resolution and justice for others. We believe, however that for this society to move on those who have suffered from violence must find appropriate places for their voices to be heard and that care should be taken to ensure that those who have suffered have a say in the purpose and shape of any mechanism for reconciliation. Chances of successful resolution will be enhanced when other, complementary processes are also involved such as the organisation of support services, the use of other legal processes to seek redress and help people who have suffered to understand their role in examining the past.

Summary

This chapter began by describing the major flaws which afflicted the original inquiry into Bloody Sunday. The Widgery Tribunal had a much too narrow focus and its terms of reference were constricted by political and security force concerns. The Tribunal's procedures were sometimes injudicious and many of the conclusions which Widgery drew were inconsistent with the limited evidence presented. It is difficult to find any defence of these flaws, over 30 years after the Report was published, save that the exigencies of the time and the crisis of state led to such an incomplete and inadequate review of the events of the day. There seems little doubt that, in the decades which followed, the families' traumatic experiences were reinforced and prolonged because of the continuing sense of injustice which flowed from the process and conclusions of the Widgery Tribunal.

Conversely, the social and political context which immediately preceded the establishment and running of the Saville Inquiry was much more conducive to an open, transparent process to which various constituencies could commit themselves. The Inquiry was set up a full four years after the first paramilitary ceasefires in Northern Ireland and at a time when renewed attempts were being made to establish a power sharing political administration in Belfast for the first time since 1973. The Inquiry was carried out in a time of relative peace; during these six years many attempts were made by local, national and international politicians to resolve the outstanding causes of the conflict. These circumstances created a more optimistic environment which helped build confidence in the work of the Saville Inquiry, aided no doubt by the rigour and independence of its work.

[154]

Nonetheless the Inquiry has been criticised by some Bloody Sunday family members, observers and the wider public. There has been almost universal criticism about the perceived excessive costs paid to lawyers over the long period of the Inquiry. Delays caused by appeals made by the soldiers and the Appeal Court's decision to allow anonymity for the security forces has weakened some family members' confidence in the Inquiry. There is also a realisation that, despite the unearthing of a great deal of evidence, those who carried out the killings may not be convicted of any crime. It is also very unrealistic to expect the Inquiry to entirely resolve the question about guilt, culpability and reparation for the families. The Inquiry was not designed as a truth and reconciliation commission, nor has there been adequate social and therapeutic support for family members and other who have had to sit through these long years of listening to witnesses, reading evidence and awaiting the outcome of the Inquiry. These are issues that are outwith its remit, but which are in need of resolution in future arrangements for services and help for the Bloody Sunday families. These points are taken up in the concluding chapter.

10 Witnessing Saville

In this chapter, we present the unfolding of the inquiry process, reactions to testimony, family members' perceptions of the process, and their hopes and fears for the outcome. The inquiry has provided an opportunity not only for many family members to tell their stories about Bloody Sunday, but also for them to learn about the experiences of others that day. Group sharing and realising the universality of experience validated many family and community members' feelings.

Testimony: giving and getting support

People testified and family members thanked them for enduring that 'daunting experience'. While it was difficult to hear the stories of others, family members felt less isolated, and supported others who testified and who were 'going through murderdom'. One man who had never talked about his experience, 'cried like a baby' because he believed he was a coward, guilty for 29 years with 'no right to talk' about his experience. He did not stop to help others, but ran away from the shooting and he survived. A family member was extremely empathic in her response to his testimony:

> I feel so sorry for them, 'cause as I says to him, 'You have no call whatsoever to feel like a coward or to feel guilty. You had to run for your life out there'. Being a family member, I can fully understand it.... It's so great for a lot of people in the town, that it has given them that opportunity for the first time to talk about it.

Managing the day-to-day business of the inquiry for the families and community has required an intensive commitment. Advocacy and assisting others are important in resolving trauma and some family members acted as liaison to other family members. They alternated time between the Guildhall where the inquiry was taking place and the Bloody Sunday Centre located across the town square from the Guildhall because they believe it was important for someone to be in the Guildhall and for someone to be at the Centre, 'simply for the families or for people coming in and inquiring'. They worked with the families and assured them that someone would be available for problem solving or to help as events unfolded as the inquiry progressed. Family members also dealt with the media, tourists and educational groups.

At other times, their role involved supporting those who were about to give testimony and who were anxious, fearful and 'likely to be overcome' during the process. Supporting others, including other family members, was challenging and anxiety provoking, because, as a family member explained:

> Everybody feels the pain for each other, because they are all very supportive of each other. …You say to yourself 'What do I do here? Put my arm around them? Try and help them?' Or whatever and you try and look after them.

Sometimes witnesses were extremely worried and 'under a lot of pressure' before they testified, so family members tried to calm them and then rejoiced with them in their palpable relief when they finished:

> The expression on their faces before they go in and the expression on their faces when they come out is totally different. It's like 'Aaaaah, it's over'. I feel relief for them that they have given their story. … It's taken nearly 30 years to tell their stories, which they have been denied all these years. The fear within the witnesses is quite simply that they don't want to let the families down. They want to go in and tell the truth, and every one is telling the truth.

Some family members appreciated having a 'a wee safety net', a place such as the Bloody Sunday Centre that set aside areas away from the main lobby where they could take a break. They found that moving to a different environment and having some-one to talk to was helpful, particularly someone who could help them to clarify issues. They could have a 'wee cup of tea' with-out having to go elsewhere in town. Family members went to the Centre for catharsis after testimony was complete for the day, and 'sort of recked [discussed] it and threw it about': 'I was raging when he said such and such', or 'Is this right?' or 'Is this wrong?' They could then go home and 'be a wee bit, you know, not too bad'.

Experiencing the Inquiry day by day

The Inquiry was 'interesting, but difficult ... a lot going on' and family members experienced 'sheer frustration' with what seemed to be irrelevant questions such as 'Did you see shooting?' As a family member remarked contemptuously, 'People didn't stand about to see shooting, people run. You might have heard shooting but nobody was actually looking to see who was shooting at them, you know'. Another family member commented proudly, 'I think I could nearly be a lawyer at the end of it, because you learn so much' listening to and learning all the 'big words', legal jargon, which they had never heard before. The inquiry was also 'very enlightening at times' with 'people telling the truth in their own way', whether they were 'more educated people' or 'ordinary persons in the street'. The testimonies of Bishop Daly and schoolmasters were 'good to listen to ... precise'. The 'ordinary' people had more difficulty, were more easily 'put off their track'. If they had seen something, 'it did not seem to be coming over as clear'.

One man found the inquiry very exciting at the beginning because he felt that they were going to have the truth at last, but then he began to feel that 'it wasn't as clear cut. It's very frustrating, at times it's boring because you are hearing the same material over and over again'. He also found the soldiers' representatives to be 'obnoxious' at times. He realised that they were 'doing their jobs' and the soldiers were 'entitled to representation', but felt that they treaded 'on spots that are very tender'. He knew he must deal with his feelings about the soldiers' versions of events, but sometimes, he admitted, the urge to shout was strong. Shouting was not the answer, he acknowledged, but it was 'difficult to accept what's going to be said here, to hold your nerve. This is the nature of the animal. It's hurtful. I'd be emotional from time to time but I'd be fairly guarded'.

Hearing about the last moments of the dead

Several family members attended the inquiry daily and sometimes had difficulty sitting 'listening to evidence ... some of it is pretty blunt. ... There's a lot of emotion there, a lot of crying. We have been brought to tears and many, many times, it didn't really matter who it was they were talking about'. While listening was difficult, it was tolerable until 'mention of something pulls at you. There but for the grace of God, go I. It could've been me.' When the testimony was about their own relative, they 'fell to pieces'.

At times testimonies or evidence family members expected were 'going to be a jolt or a shock, weren't', and then 'something totally unrelated or insignificant' was unnerving. Seeing photographs of bodies being carried out or hearing witnesses talk about 'a dead brother ... whoever shot him and how he tried to claw his way in through the doors' was incredibly distressing. A family member pictured his brother 'falling to the ground and people running over lifting him and stuff like that. If you go through them all individually, you can actually picture everyone, how they met their end, and how they were injured.'

It was painful to hear members of other families testify about their feelings for the dead son or father, 'how he was so much cared for, how they missed him, things they have held on to, belonging to him'. The testimonies were about the 'forceful taking of a human being's life, somebody who was loved and who was full of love and joy and that hurt'. One family member became very angry as she listened to testimony because her brother's death was reduced to a statistic. She responded angrily, 'The loss of humanity is not seen there, the wanton destructive act, the murder that took place isn't seen. It becomes a game and that at times hurts.'

One woman, who saw footage of the shootings for the first time and without advance notice, recognised her father as he waved his arms in the air in a futile gesture as he attempted to stop the soldiers from firing. She watched him as he was shot, fell to the ground and rose up again, waving his arms in desperation. She was dismayed:

> There was an army personnel jeep or whatever it was, with
> a red cross on it. They could have helped my father and

they could have helped my brother. They could have come up to the barricade and they didn't. At no time did any soldier on the day help any of the wounded, any of the dead, or anybody that was hysterical because of what they witnessed.

Questions answered

Listening to eyewitness accounts and viewing film footage was a very traumatising process, but it was helpful and healing because clouds of confusion about what had happened on Bloody Sunday began to dissipate. This state of confusion, compounded by years of silence and fear during the Troubles in Northern Ireland, it can be argued, was partly responsible for the tenacity of trauma symptoms family members continued to experience. People were, for the first time, 'getting questions answered' that were always in the 'back of their minds'. They often wondered, 'Did he speak to anybody before he died? What were his last words? Where was he seen? What kind of mood was he in?' One man, as he listened to the testimony of those who had been at the scene of the shootings on Bloody Sunday, gained new insights about his father. He realised for the first time that his father was a hero that day by trying to protect three of the wounded, including his own son. He had never considered his father in that light:

> When my father went to the barricades, he went through the middle of the three bodies and he just pulled the three bodies together. He wasn't just in there for his son. He was out there for the three people who were lying mortally wounded at the barricades. When I heard this, I realised after so many years my father was one of the many heroes that went to the assistance of people. I found that very hard, the fact that I didn't include him as one of those particular heroes in Derry that day.

One woman, horrified for years after Bloody Sunday at the manner the army handled the bodies of some of the deceased that day, was particularly resentful that soldiers had prevented a priest from giving the last rites of the church to the dying. She learned that the priest had persisted, and her brother did actually receive the sacrament. She found this very comforting. Another family member found the testimony of strangers about her brother upsetting, but also validating. People traced his movements throughout the march. There were also many photographs of him as the march progressed. She was convinced that this testimony fully exonerated her brother who had been considered by the Widgery Tribunal to be a nail bomber:

> He's doing absolutely nothing. He looks very happy in all the photographs of him. I can't believe how many photographs there is of him and at the time of Widgery the conclusion was he was lurking in the background with something sinister in mind. Now it's obvious he was not lurking in the background because there is too many photographs of him.

A woman who was always willing to give the soldiers the 'benefit of the doubt' that perhaps her brother had been 'mistakenly shot', learned the details. Listening to testimony was very difficult for her, but she reversed her position, she said, 'knowing now what I know about the attitude of soldiers'. Another family member gained fresh insight about some events that happened at the time of the funerals. She remembered vividly 'thousands of people and they were standing on rooftops, tops of cars lined to the Creggan'. She was dismayed afterwards, at their silence, when she felt they 'really didn't care at all'. They seemed indifferent, as if 'it never happened' in the months and years after Bloody Sunday. She finally learned the reason:

> At the time I thought there were a wild lot of people that cared, but after Bloody Sunday I thought people don't care at all because they don't talk about it. They didn't talk about it at school. Because of the inquiry, the most positive thing that I have learned is the reason for that was that the people of Derry also tried to protect the families. They thought that by not talking about it would help. They thought that was their way of protecting the

families. They didn't want to put them under any more stress than they were already under.

She asked well-known people in the community who never visited her mother and father after her brother was killed, 'Why did you never approach my family and tell them what you have just said in there?' Repeatedly the response was, 'the pain that you were going through was enough, and we didn't want to put you through any more pain'. The inquiry, she believed, was not just for the families, but for community members as well:

> This was their opportunity as well, letting the families know and the world know what they witnessed on that day. It was also relieving them because it was something that they couldn't talk about themselves.

This misguided collusion of silence, however, did not protect the families, nor community members who were really protecting themselves by not talking to the families. The silence perpetuated the trauma of the families and the community at large.

'Taking time out'

Family members sometimes had to 'take time out ... to walk away from it some days'. One man decreased the extent of his attendance at the inquiry sessions, because, he explained, 'I knew it was affecting me in relationships with my own family.' Some family members were unable 'get through the evidence without a fag [cigarette] in their hand' but they hoped by the time the inquiry concludes, that they will 'finally be able to put some closure' on that part of their lives. They always knew 'that there wasn't going to be an easy path'. They knew 'that certain obstacles were going to be thrown' before them, and that it would be the 'easiest option, just to stand away'; however, they always went back for more. Whatever happens, they pledged, they will 'press on' and 'go back'. They felt that they 'owed it' to their dead brother. A family member vowed, 'They'll have to take me out of there in an old overcoat.' Although the process was so difficult, affecting them and their families so much, and so upsetting, family members believed, as one man summed it up decisively,

'If it goes down in history that my brother was not a gunman, he was totally innocent of any crime, then it's worth it.' They are 'determined to get to the truth', otherwise, they believe, Bloody Sunday cannot be resolved.

Repudiating Widgery

The families have always perceived the conclusions of the Widgery Tribunal after Bloody Sunday as unjust, viewing it as a 'cover-up' and victim blaming. These perceptions have most certainly contributed to the degree and tenacity of posttraumatic stress. The families hoped guardedly that the outcomes of the Saville Inquiry will be different. They prayed that all evidence will be heard and that their position will be validated. In spite of the difficulties involved in listening to testimony, family members felt that the story of Bloody Sunday was being told in a 'truthful manner. ... The truth's slowly but surely coming to the front and the whole world's watching'. They believed that 'Widgery is on trial.' They wanted it 'dead and buried' and the British government to get past the accepted notion, 'their boys wouldn't do any wrong'. The Widgery Tribunal was, they were convinced, 'all more or less behind closed doors, it was all done and dusted before Widgery even sat down. ... He did what he was told to do and that is to lay the blame outside the paras.'

Repudiation of the Widgery Tribunal has been a long time goal of the Bloody Sunday Justice Campaign, and family members believed that they 'have succeeded in that. He [Widgery] has been blown out of the water, in a manner of speaking'. Had the Widgery Tribunal been more thoughtful and thorough, and the truth found at that time, family members believed not so many lives would have been lost over the years. The sister of a man killed alleged:

> There was a lot of people died in the name of Bloody Sunday, which should not have been allowed to happen. I feel that Widgery is totally responsible for that. We shouldn't be having to sit and go through what we are going through now. That should have been done then. God have mercy on that man. I don't know how he can rest in his grave, I really don't.

Family members hoped that the outcome of the Saville Inquiry will lead to acknowledging the 'truth of the innocence' of their loved ones, 'people who were murdered' because they were 'labelled', as 'nail bombers' and 'gunmen' and, they believe, 'It's so important that that's taken away from them'. They wanted acknowledgement of guilt, not only from the soldiers, but also from the political establishment, prosecutions of those found guilty and 'acknowledgement of the fact that the paras came in and murdered people without any justification whatsoever ... a truth that has been known for 29 years. ... The world and its mother knows the truth.'

Fairness of the process: hopes and fears

Family members held mixed views about the inquiry process. They experienced both 'good days and bad days'. The longer the inquiry process goes on, the more cynicism and mistrust some experience:

> It's so typical of them. It's what you expect. Those representing the Brits are going to try and muddy the waters here and there, and they're going to try and create more grey areas. They're going to try and always throw the question mark over maybe why their soldiers were under pressure to open fire.

Some family members were upset because a good deal of material was not yet available to the inquiry, '1,000 missing photographs', but others were incredibly surprised that they have been able to make new friends among members of the inquiry team, a 'lovely' experience :

> They have seen us as ordinary human beings the same as themselves. They have seen us for what we are, family members, you know. At first we were afraid to talk to them because we didn't know if we were allowed to talk to them. Eventually being Derry people I mean, the craic [good time] we have with them is really good. Just all a bit of friendly banter, which is something I didn't think we would ever have been able to do with them.

Many family members believed that Judge Saville was fair, and had a 'good deal of faith that Saville was 'trying to do his best', but that his 'hands are tied' to some extent, that the inquiry is not really an independent one, but was governed by the British establishment. They felt that Saville 'has not been given the promised independence that he is entitled'. The issue of testimony by the soldiers involved in the shooting on Bloody Sunday was a 'sensitive' one, and family members believed that Judge Saville was 'trying to be fair' in deciding where the testimony should take place. They also believed that any decision Saville made would likely be overruled in London's High Court through court appeals by the soldiers' legal teams. As one family member observed, 'People don't realise that because Saville makes a ruling, that ruling doesn't necessarily stick because it'll go to the Court of Appeal, so it will be overruled at the end of the day.'

A family member who was not 'totally positive' about the inquiry experienced times when he 'is filled with hope, that this is going the correct road'. He felt sometimes 'there could be a resolution here of this whole situation', but most often he felt 'suspicious, pessimistic', not enthusiastic about the outcome, and it was 'hard work ... very wearing'. He has been fighting 29 years to ascertain his brother's innocence, but, he despaired, 'Still there's no clear picture that my brother is innocent. I'm still very much aware that you have to prove your innocence, it's not that the guilty have to prove why they done it.'

Witness badgering

Family members were upset when they perceived that witnesses were being badgered in an inquiry that some believed 'has failed them'. They felt that Judge Saville has been somewhat inconsistent, 'not as strong as he should be' in protecting witnesses who were attempting to give their accounts of what happened on Bloody Sunday. One family member remarked that some people 'get really upset'. She was 'dying' to shout: 'Would you leave that witness alone!' She believed the questioning was adversarial and forced 'people into corners and they can say things that they don't mean to say'. Even Bishop Daly's day in court was 'heartbreaking.... He is such a mild man, and they kept firing these questions at him' and at the 'Knights of Malta, who would have treated anyone who needed assistance, even injured soldiers'. 'Some people when they're cross-examined they get confused' and the solicitors 'try to say then that they didn't see what they are supposed to have seen'. They felt that some witnesses were intimidated:

> More or less called 'liars' by the solicitors for the soldiers
> ... but naturally the solicitors for the soldiers are going to
> try and undermine them. People may get mixed up in rela-
> tion to their memory, it's acceptable. Saville understands
> it, and there are times he's interjected and he's cut in to
> protect the witness. Not very often, by the way.

Other family members, however, felt that most witnesses 'have been able to stand up for themselves'. They felt that there was nothing to fear 'when people were telling the truth'. They were confident that Saville would do what was necessary although it was sometimes difficult for the witnesses and 'they could be more hard-lined on them, you know'. Some witnesses were afraid that they had 'let family members down in some way' but family members deeply appreciated their efforts, the fact that witnesses tolerated 'being grilled ... an inquisitorial time' that was necessary 'to get at the truth, all the truth, not just selective truth'. Family members also believed it was important that 'the paramilitaries get in there and tell their role and what they were doing'.

In trying times during testimony, the Derry sense of humour still prevailed. A family member gleefully recalled witnessing a self-confident elderly woman on the witness stand unintimidated by the process or by legal proceedings:

> One day there was a wee woman, she must have been
> about 70 or 80, and here this clerk, he's 'Lord this' and 'My
> learned friend', and she said 'C'm'ere son, wait till I tell
> you something.'
> 'Were you at the north end of Roselyn Street?' he says.
> 'Son,' she says, 'It's like this. I was standing down at the
> bottom of Roselyn Street, it could be the north, it could be
> the south, but I was standing at the *bottom* of Roselyn
> Street and this all happened.' We're all sitting goin', 'Go

for it!' you know, because it was sheer, unadulterated truth, you know this was truth, this wasn't something that was put into this woman's mouth.

She bent over, she looked at Saville and she said, 'Mr.' Now, she had a mike at her mouth, and she lowered her voice, and she said, 'They were down the Bog to get the rubber bullets.' The Americans bought them off them for souvenirs. And Saville's sittin' like this here, 'Where is this woman coming from?' 'And how far away were you from the shooting?' 'Well, do you see where you are standing now? she asked. 'Now he could have been a wee bit further away than that.' She was a gem, you know. Some days it does be good!

Apportioning the blame

Many family members believe there will never be total justice for what happened on Bloody Sunday. As a the sister of a young man killed stated, 'Something positive may happen that they may say that all those killed on Bloody Sunday was innocent', which will conclude the proceedings and 'they [British Government] will make excuses for what they done'. However she does not think those who were killed will be 'totally exonerated', nor does she think that 'individuals will be held accountable even though it can and will be proved that it was murder'. She would like to think 'they would pay the consequences for murder but I don't think they will. It won't happen. I'm sure about that.'

Others felt there will be incredible effort to 'apportion blame all around'. As one man said, 'Now we're up to the blame game.' He had 'no great faith' in the inquiry process, that its outcome was 'already pre-determined' no matter what the truth is about 'innocence and murder'. He thought that the 'process will not go far enough', that they will not 'have the courage at this particular time'. Everyone, whether it is the British Government, the British Establishment, or solicitors for the soldiers, knew the truth, he believed, but 'they're going to try and push the blame, hoping that something falls into place where the blame can be applied to someone else apart from the paras'. He believed that the British authorities will say it was an 'illegal march', the 'soldiers were young and inexperienced', or they will blame the Civil Rights movement for 'bringing so many people on to the streets'. There will be some blame for 'some of the senior officers for a break-down in the discipline' or for bringing 'these particular troops in' but, 'at the end of the day, they brought them in, and they murdered'.

Several family members, as one woman said, have 'very little doubt' that there will be a qualified declaration of innocence for those murdered or wounded on Bloody Sunday, that they 'weren't using any firearm or legal force, but there will be an attempt to try and tarnish their reputation a little bit to excuse what they can'. British legal authorities will not retreat from the position that there were gunmen and bombers, she believed, claiming that due to the overexcited state or inexperience of the soldiers, people, their rela-tives, were killed by mistake. She believed, 'that's the line, and if that is the end result, then it's a waste to a degree of the last three and a half years'.

Even if the names of the dead are cleared, family members were pessimistic about prosecutions of those responsible for the killing, and 'people will get their names cleared, and that will be the end of it' because in other incidents in years past, 'no soldiers have ever been prosecuted'. They have been prosecuted and let out after a few years, and 'now they're back in the army again. They're not really going to attack their own soldiers, you know.'

Ultimately, family members wanted the truth, and if there is evidence that legal proceedings would follow the inquiry, they would like that process to unfold. If some people go to trial, they could 'care less whether they actually ever served any time or anything like that, but would like the judicial process to happen ... prosecutions taking place, even if they get a suspended sentence'. One woman said, however, 'If soldiers really were acting irre-sponsibility or if it's really true that they were following orders,' then they should not be 'prosecuted under those conditions,' but somebody 'should be held responsible for making that decision,' otherwise she will just have 'a deeper level of cynicism about authority'.

Another family member wanted to be certain that it is acknowledged that there was no 'conspiracy by several hundred Derry citizens', that the victims of Bloody Sunday were:

Not carrying any lethal weapon, were not carrying petrol bombs, nail bombs or firearms, that they were shot as they were fleeing the aggression of the British Security Services that day, the paratroopers, that they were deliberately gunned down.

Another family member agreed:

There's just no way they could have mistaken a gunman or a petrol bomber standing close or near or even in the same town as the person they shot. It was just pure murder. There was no justification for it.

Others believed that the British Army, the Stormont administration and the British Government decided that 'a lesson had to be taught to the Derry population and that lesson would echo around the rest of Northern Ireland and in some form or fashion they thought that would resolve their political situation'. Losing a few lives in the process was a small price to pay. Family members generally believed that the soldiers acted as a unit:

It wasn't that one guy got out of order and shot my brother. They were acting in cohesion with each other, so they were all a party to the murder whether you can identify the individual or those groups of soldiers who acted in it who were party to that murder. I'd love to see them prosecuted. But I have to accept today, with the Good Friday Agreement, they are not going to serve a day in jail.

Family members' demands for accountability at higher levels of government decision making were clear, since 'this was not just about the soldiers ... there were politicians involved', even to the level of 'Edward Heath himself' and the intelligence service that supplied information implying that 'drastic measures' were needed in Derry. As one family member noted, 'I think at the end of the day, you know, it could've been worse.' Another man hoped that higher authorities would be held accountable for their actions:

> But not only the soldiers, I think it goes higher than the
> soldiers. I think it came out of Whitehall, high in Whitehall
> in London. I just don't know. If it went all the way to
> Heath, you wouldn't know that because there seemed to
> be a lack of anything down on paper to tie anybody down
> to anything.

New political arrangements in Northern Ireland, between the
British and Irish Governments, have indicated that the British
Government and its forces would not pursue paramilitary fugi-
tives. 'That's sad,' a family member commented, because he had
worked so many years for justice for his brother. He vowed he
would 'make a personal decision' about what would be acceptable
to him 'in the light of a peace settlement in Northern Ireland, you
know in Ireland as a whole. ... It might be a price we'll have to
pay.' Furthermore, he asserted, he knew that the only positive
outcome of a resolution of the Bloody Sunday tragedy, is 'to
enforce in law that it can't happen to other people'. He added, 'I
don't want anybody to go through that again. And the only way
you can guarantee that is when people that are responsible are
brought to task. Now that doesn't mean there has to be imprison-
ment,' but, he added, there must be an acknowledgement 'that
you are out on license as a murderer, what you did was wrong'.
The assignment of responsibility was the most important aspect
for him in resolving the emotional impact of Bloody Sunday. If
this happens, then his 'brother's life was not in vain'.

Another man talked about his past desire for revenge and
anger, 'but he is no longer angry at the soldiers'. He wanted a
straightforward declaration of innocence: 'All Blair had to do was
turn round and say that "these people are innocent", forget about
word play and tell us that we as family members can consider
them to be innocent. He has got to say, "They are innocent
people."' This family member also wanted prosecutions, but not
jail sentences for those found guilty:

> At the end of the day, if you've got innocence, there's guilt,
> so what do you do in relation to the guilty people? I don't
> know. I certainly don't want to see anybody between 60 or
> 70 years of age going into prison. At least what should be

[170]

done is that they should be charged with the offence, if we can pin them to that offence. If we can charge them, and then we can let it be known within their own community 'here is a person who was charged and convicted of murder'. He's a murderer, it's as simple as that there, and let him live within his own community, don't put him in jail. That'll do me. I would be quite satisfied with that.

For another family member, 'justice is an important factor within this process'. He could not tolerate the fact such young people:

> ... all young boys, just about to start their lives, and to put it really crudely, the bastards came in and ruined it and walked away, and laughed about killing. Now these guys were psychopaths, I don't care what the British Government says.

He believed that one soldier was responsible for three deaths and 'this guy walked away and was never ever brought to justice'. For him, it's important that all the killers, all paras be brought to justice, particularly Soldier F who:

> ... went in that day with intent to kill people and he didn't give a damn who he shot and went away as if nothing happened, and gave a statement that says he remembers coming to Derry and leaving Derry but 84 times in his statement he says he does not recall ...

The family member felt the testimony of Soldier F was a 'mockery', and 'if that's not a sign of guilt, what is there? This guy is still in the same frame of mind as he was that day. He doesn't give a shit about human life.'

'It's worth it'

In spite of family members' guarded optimism, a degree of pessimism and cynicism about the inquiry process and outcome, and the pain, frustration and difficulties in the everyday testimony, most agreed that the work to achieve the inquiry has been worth it:

Oh God, aye, every minute, every minute ... [in order to] achieve truth and justice for those who died and for acceptance of the truth, not just for the families, but for the British Government, the Unionist Community, and for everyone.

They hoped that the inquiry will find 'all our people to be innocent', a priority. Family members acknowledged they had a 'long way to go and hoped they will be able to see it through', because they believe they 'owe it' to their brothers, and 'everybody else who died that day'. A family member promised that he 'personally will weather whatever they throw at us'.

Family members insisted they have to 'get this right this time', because, as one man sadly said, 'I have nothing more to give, you know. It has got to be this time or that's it, because I'm finished.' He worried about the future and what he will do after the inquiry concludes, regardless of the outcome. He wondered, 'What am I going to do, say five years down the line? How am I going to fill my days? I just don't know. That would be my main concern. I don't know whether I need counselling, what you call a professional counsellor.' Another woman thought that if the inquiry does not accomplish the goals the families sought, it would be like going into 'a black hole, a bottomless depression'. She thought that 'some people put their hopes too high and they're going to come down'.

Summary

During the day to day unfolding of the inquiry process, family members hoped, yet feared the outcomes. Attending the inquiry was exhausting, yet necessary for healing, validating, worth the effort and pain involved in listening to testimony. If justice is not served in the manner family members hope, or if they perceive any duplicity in the process, not only will the processing of their loved one's death continue to be traumatic, we believe it will likely be compounded. Family members have an abiding belief that full disclosure of the truth and providing all parties an opportunity to be heard at the inquiry will vindicate them. Even if their goals are achieved, the quest for justice has taken a toll.

Some people will continue with the cause if needed, others will drop out. Some family members, particularly those who have been most involved, will most likely need intensive social service intervention. Their lives and identity have been defined by this quest for many years.

11 Conclusion

The research upon which much of this book is based began at the time of the 25th anniversary of Bloody Sunday in 1997 and continued as a follow-up study at the time of the 30th anniversary in 2002. Using a primarily qualitative approach, we explored the experience of trauma and its consequences for a sample of Bloody Sunday family members in as many of their own words as possible. In the course of *Bloody Sunday: Trauma, Pain and Politics* a variety of themes emerged about the views and experiences of families who have suffered as a result of this catastrophic incident over 30 years ago. Their pain can be related to silence engendered by fear, victim blaming, ongoing exposure to violence and intimidation, lack of adequate social and health service care, and the interaction between experiences of violent death, grief and trauma. In particular there was anger at the perceived injustice about what happened on Bloody Sunday and the failure of the Widgery Tribunal to deal with those who were responsible for the killings. This longstanding grievance was one of the many factors which hindered trauma resolution for family members. In this concluding chapter we wish to draw these themes together and make some modest suggestions for the future health and well being of the families.

Issues of methodology

It is important to acknowledge that, although a range of approaches are available in the field of trauma research, we have tried to make the case for the use of a primarily qualitative methodology, supported by two quantitative measures. These methods help support our view that many of the people who were interviewed continue to experience symptoms of posttraumatic stress, grief, and feelings of guilt and anger about Bloody Sunday. There may have been other reasons why participants were psychologically distressed at the time of the 25th anniversary, for example ongoing violence caused by the Troubles throughout these years. Conversely it is also likely that some individuals found healthy resolutions to the trauma such as belonging to the Bloody Sunday Justice Campaign or achieving autonomy through access to higher education or economic success. Some benefited from effective parenting methods that modelled positive coping skills such as determination, persistence and maintenance of self-dignity in the face of adversity. Yet we still wish to argue that our findings suggest that a relationship exists between the general emotional health of this group and PTSD symptoms resulting from the Bloody Sunday trauma.

This study use a primarily qualitative method and no generalisations can be made to the wider circle of family members who may also have been traumatised; it was a 'snapshot' of what was happening in twelve of the 14 families affected by the death of a relative on Bloody Sunday. The study was not designed to explore the other very important experiences of those wounded on the day; their views are often excluded in the growing literature and are of course important in this context. It may be that those who were injured may now be ready to tell their stories. Many family members who participated in the study were concerned about the future of their children and were fearful that their pain might be transmitted to the next generation. Families are often close knit in Derry, and several generations of families live in close proximity to one another. Conversations with some of the children of those who participated in the study indicated that they too were affected by the events and aftermath of Bloody Sunday, having lived with traumatised parents. Further research into the intergenerational consequences of trauma among these family members is warranted. It would be important to learn how subsequent generations experience living with traumatised persons and how vicariously traumatised persons navigate their parents' world of pain and politics.

Complex trauma: implications for resolution

What we have concluded, using the research approach in this study, is that events before, during and after Bloody Sunday have likely contributed to a complex, persistent, and debilitating Type 2 trauma for many family members. Type 2 trauma reactions are responses to ongoing trauma over many years, and often are experienced by persons who were repeatedly abused as children, combat veterans or by those who live in a war zone. Type 2 trauma is much more severe and resistant to treatment than a Type 1 trauma, a response to a single catastrophic event, that tends to have a more favourable outcome and is more amenable to treatment. In many ways the Bloody Sunday family members tended to respond to the event and its aftermath not unlike adult victims of childhood sexual abuse and, like these victims, the scars are chronic and the pain unremitting. The abusive caretaker in this case, it can be argued, is the British government, which in family members' perceptions, has blamed the victim, distorted the facts, and continued to perpetuate the abuse. As with child victims, the Bloody Sunday families had no recourse but to suffer in silence for many years.

Fear and a disempowered generation

One of the features of the research findings which informed this book was that many of the respondents had not told their story before. At the time of the first stage of interviews few respondents had been asked to talk about their trauma, nor did they appear to trust their story to others outside the community and immediate families. Perhaps this can be explained in terms of fear for their safety, and that of other family members. Once asked, however, many family members were able to recount their feelings and experiences, and these narratives about the events of Bloody Sunday were commonly related in a highly detailed, hypnotic manner, a typical feature of chronic traumatic stress. Family members told stories of subsequent unremitting house raids by the security forces and harassment by police and security forces on the streets. They generally thought that this was due to their relationship with alleged terrorists (those killed). For many family members the mere sight of armoured vehicles or troops on the streets engendered fear and panic and triggered flashbacks and other intrusions related to Bloody Sunday. It was probable that fear and intimidation by the security forces impacted on trauma integration and contributed to a chronic state of hyper-vigilance and phobic avoidance. Republican politicisation of the families' tragedy and recurring media accounts tended to cause upset, particularly at the times of the anniversary.

The 25th anniversary, a symbolic milestone, however, may have created a propitious environment for telling the story. This period coincided with important shifts in politics and society leading to the peace process in Northern Ireland. At the same time groups like the Bloody Sunday Justice Campaign provided family members with local, community based support and empowered them to seek help and justice. It may be that victims and survivors of the Troubles may now and in the future be encouraged to tell their stories in a relatively safe environment.

The human experience of trauma: loss

We have argued throughout this book that we can only begin to understand such violent events and their traumatic aftermath by setting the event in its political and historical context as well as making sense of other relevant existing literature, including debates about theories on posttraumatic stress and grief. Of particular interest to the authors were the human experiences related to the trauma of Bloody Sunday and the significance attributed to this event by the families affected by the death of a sibling or parent that day. The inability to resolve trauma among the Bloody Sunday families is consistent with the literature on PTSD, particularly the interaction between the concepts of trauma and grief in children and adolescents. The narratives indicated that children tended to be overlooked during the aftermath of Bloody Sunday and left to their own resources to deal with their feelings, confusion, chaos, and lack of information. In some cases siblings and children of those killed lost their opportunity to grow up 'normally'. In the aftermath of Bloody Sunday parents who were interviewed were often not emotionally and physically available for their children. Many were 'parentified' and required to assume adult responsibilities in large families. Some parents of family members were emotionally absent and lost as 'parents' to their children thereafter. Several parents of family members in this study also suffered poor health after the event and some died shortly afterwards. Some mothers were continually grieving, and one had amnesia for five years following Bloody Sunday. Some fathers also drank heavily. These losses seem particularly important, given the closely-knit nature of family and community life in

Derry. It may be that such loss can never be fully resolved, because 'nothing was ever the same again'.

All family members in this study appeared to have their identities compromised by the close association with the trauma. This may be the result of the process of internalisation of thoughts and feelings about the event or, perhaps, the impact of external factors such as community perceptions and expectations of the families. A tremendous sense of loss around the relative's death was experienced by all family members. The loss was seen to have cataclysmic consequences as family members alluded to the never to be born children of victims, the 'broken family chain', the loss of the future. This loss extends to the community at large and remains fixed in the collective memory of the city of Derry, even among those who were born much later. A variety of other losses also emerged in the narrative material including the loss of family celebrations such as birthdays and wedding anniversaries, loss of faith, health and well being, loss of trust and loss of innocence in the face of violence and perceived betrayal.

A normal funeral

Respondents spontaneously recounted stories of family deaths and 'normal' funerals as a means to inform us about the differences between these events and that of Bloody Sunday. They even included humorous anecdotes about family members, ghost stories, and pranks played at funerals. Although coping with other deaths was always difficult, family members felt, however, that they grieved appropriately at those times and were able to move on. In the case of the deaths caused by Bloody Sunday the grieving process is incomplete, complicated, and perhaps for some, not begun. Funeral rituals tended to be abnormal or absent; there was no 'Irish Wake' and parents and other family members of the victims suffered endlessly. As family members frequently explained, one can grieve a natural death, but not a violent one that is followed by victim blaming.

Justice, violence and politics

Other themes that emerged were those of need for justice and tolerance within a framework of anti-violence and apoliticism.

Some family members even appeared to be willing to forgive the individual soldier who killed their relative, but were not so generous in forgiving the British government. Seeking justice for the dead relative through confronting the government, something that could be construed as political activity, was not the same as being involved in other political issues of the day. Most participants adopted an anti-violent, apolitical stance. They tended not to want to inflict their pain on anyone else. Their values emerged from a fear of the consequences of their own anger and concern that this would infect their children, most of whom were born years later. Respondents seemed to make a deliberate choice not to discuss Bloody Sunday with their children because they believed that silence afforded a means to protect them. Family members did not want their children to become bitter or to seek revenge through paramilitary activity. They did not want to endanger their children or suffer the loss of another family member. Some family members, however, did tell their children about Bloody Sunday as a way of illustrating what could happen by being in the wrong place at the wrong time.

30 years after Bloody Sunday

At the time of the second phase of the research – the 30th anniversary – family members reported that the previous five years had been a stressful, yet important and productive time for them. There appeared to be a new atmosphere of openness about discussing Bloody Sunday, not only in the families but also in the general Derry community. Despite the difficulties and obstacles which emerged as a result of legal processes which slowed the Saville Inquiry, respondents generally felt that the Inquiry process, while painful, may be a necessary part of a process of trauma resolution. They were understandably concerned about the possibility that the Saville Inquiry might not deliver 'truth and justice'. This of course depended on whether the Inquiry process and ultimate conclusion is perceived as just, particularly regarding soldiers' testimony and how the state managed this process. The worry and expectation might be that these possible outcomes will compound the original trauma of Bloody Sunday.

It is also very unrealistic to expect the Inquiry to entirely resolve the question about guilt, culpability and reparation for the families. The Inquiry was not designed as a truth and reconciliation commission, nor has there been adequate social and therapeutic support for family members and others who have had to sit through these long years of listening to witnesses, reading evidence and awaiting the outcome. These are issues that are outside the remit of the Inquiry, but which are in need of resolution in future arrangements for services and help for the Bloody Sunday families. The Inquiry, however, is an opportunity to make things right if findings are viewed to be fair and unbiased; if this is the case then Widgery will be repudiated, an important goal of the families. A consensus seems to have emerged that the British government must act on the recommendations of the Saville Inquiry and anything less will deepen the distrust and sense of betrayal, further compounding the trauma.

It also has to be recognised, however, that this legal process, in itself, may be only partly helpful for some Bloody Sunday family members, and must be viewed in the context of wider social and political processes in Northern Ireland. These families, like many others who have suffered as a result of the Troubles in Northern Ireland, have complex and exceptional needs. We have made the case that, historically, such groups have not received the resources and help they require to deal with their trauma, and it is only in recent years that the state is beginning to engage in this difficult area. If services are to be organised and delivered in the future then this must be carried out in partnership with local groups and communities. It is difficult to be prescriptive about such services, but they must be flexible, varied to deal with a range of different social and health needs, non-stigmatising and yet effective and regulated.

Even the development of comprehensive, well-funded services will probably not be sufficient in themselves to address all of the issues which have been raised by family members in this book. The history of the conflict in Northern Ireland has left so many deep wounds in the minds as well as the bodies of people that mechanisms need to be developed to allow for some form of collective healing about the past. This may only happen when social, economic and political conditions allow for it, and when this society comes to a point in wishing to acknowledge and reflect on each others' pain in an open and non-threatening environment. Ultimately, the resolution of trauma may only take place in the context of the current changing political processes in Northern Ireland. The Saville Inquiry into Bloody Sunday gave family members guarded hope; they are looking for a resolution that will allow them to finally have the 'Irish Wake' and begin the grief process that will eventually help them to put this trauma to rest. Once the trauma is addressed, and justice is served, it opens the possibility for the resolution of grief to begin.

In concluding this book, it is important to recognise the unfinished business that remains to be carried out by the state and citizens in Northern Ireland. There seems little doubt that we are living through a period of conflict resolution in which many individuals and groups are struggling to make sense of the profound trauma of the last decade. We wish to be modest about what we believe our contribution has been. We have focused on a specific group of families who suffered a particular trauma and ongoing sense of betrayal in which the state is explicitly implicated. There are many other people who have also suffered and whose voices need also to be heard. We also acknowledge that the various ways of carrying out research in this field are contested, as are interventions designed to help people traumatised by political violence. This is a rapidly changing and developing area and we hope that some of what we have said resonates with other research going on now and in the future.

Most importantly, the final message we wish to leave for the reader is to register our heartfelt thanks to the family members for allowing us to carry out the interviews and for trusting us with their stories. We believe that they have many needs which may only be resolved if and when the Saville Inquiry locates responsibility for Bloody Sunday with the state and those who carried out the killings, and when individuals and families are provided with adequate support and resources to begin to rebuild shattered lives.

Bibliography

American Psychiatric Association (1980). *Diagnostic and Statistical Manual of Mental Disorders (3rd ed.) DSM-III*. Washington, D.C.: American Psychiatric Association.

American Psychiatric Association (1994). *Diagnostic and Statistical Manual of Mental Disorders (4th ed.) DSM-IV*. Washington, D.C.: American Psychiatric Association.

Amnesty International (2004). *Amnesty International Report 2004*. London: Amnesty International Publications.

Aron, A. (1992). 'Testimonio, a bridge between psychotherapy and socio-therapy', *Women and Therapy*. Binghamton, NY: Haworth Press, 173–89.

Arthur, P. (1974). *The People's Democracy 1968–73*. Belfast: Blackstaff.

Ayalon, O. and Soskis, D. (eds) (1986). 'Survivors of terrorist victimisation: a follow-up study', in N. Milgram (ed.), *Stress and Coping in Time of War: Generalizations from the Israeli Experience*. New York: Brunner-Mazel, 257–74.

Banks, M., Clegg, C., Jackson, P., Kemp, N., Stafford, E. and Wall, T. (1980). 'The use of the General Health Questionnaire as an indicator of mental health in occupational studies', *Journal of Occupational Psychology*, 53: 187–94.

Bardon, J. (1992). *A History of Ulster*. Belfast: Blackstaff.

Bell, P., Kee, M., Loughrey, G., Roddy, R. and Curran, P. (1988). 'Posttraumatic stress in Northern Ireland', *Acta Psychiatrica Scandinavia*, 77, 166–9.

Bew, P., Gibbon, P. and Patterson, H. (1996). *Northern Ireland 1921–1994: Political Forces and Social Classes*. London: Serif.

Birrell, C. and Murie, A. (1980). *Policy and Government in Northern Ireland: Lessons of Devolution*. Dublin: Gill and Macmillan.

Blease, M. (1983). 'Maladjusted schoolchildren in a Belfast centre', in J. Harbison (ed.), *Children of the 'Troubles': Children in Northern Ireland*. Belfast: Stranmillis College Learning Resources Centre.

Bloody Sunday Trust (2004). www.bloodysundaytrust.org.

Bloomfield, K. (1994). *Stormont in Crisis*. Belfast: Blackstaff.

Bolton, D. (1996). 'When a community grieves: the Remembrance Day bombing, Enniskillen', in *NISW Journeys of Experience*. London: NISW.

Borooah, V. (1993). 'Northern Ireland: Typology of a regional economy', in P. Teague (ed.), *The Economy of Northern Ireland: Perspectives for Structural Change*. London: Lawrence and Wishart.

Brom, D. and Kleber, R. (1989). 'Prevention of posttraumatic stress disorder', *Journal of Traumatic Stress*, 2(3), 235–351.

Cairns, E. (1988). 'Social class, psychological well-being and minority status in Northern Ireland', *International Journal of Social Psychiatry*, 35(3), 231–6.

Cairns, E. (1989). 'Social identity and inter-group conflict in Northern Ireland: A developmental perspective', in J. Harbison (ed.), *Growing up in Northern Ireland*. Belfast: Universities Press.

Cairns, E. and Darby, J. (1998). 'The conflict in Northern Ireland: causes, consequences and controls', *American Psychologist*, 53, 754–60.

Cairns, E. and Dawes, A. (1996). 'Children: ethnic and political violence: a commentary', *Child Development*, 67, 129–39.

Cairns, E. and Lewis, C. (1999). 'Memories for political violence and mental health', *British Journal of Psychology*, 90, 25–33.

Cairns, E. and Wilson, R. (1984). 'The impact of political violence on mild psychiatric morbidity in Northern Ireland', *British Journal of Psychiatry*, 145, 631–5.

Cairns, E. and Wilson, R. (1989). 'Coping with political violence in Northern Ireland', *Social Science & Medicine*, 28(6), 621–4.

Campbell, J. (1986). *The Concept of Violence: An Examination of its Ideological Uses*, Chapter 6. Unpublished PhD thesis. Belfast: Queen's University.

Campbell, J. and Healey, A. (1999). '"Whatever you say, say something": the education, training and practice of mental health social workers in Northern Ireland', *Social Work Education*, 18(4), 389–400.

Campbell, J. and McLaughlin, J. (2000). 'The "joined-up" management of adult health and social care in Northern Ireland: lessons for the rest of the UK?', *Managing Community Care*, 8(5), 6–13.

Campbell, J. and Pinkerton, J. (1997). 'Embracing change as opportunity: reflections on social work from a Northern Ireland perspective', in B. Lesnik (ed.), *Change in Social Work*. Aldershot: Avebury.

Campbell, K. J. (2001). *Genocide and the Global Village*. Basingstoke: Palgrave.

Central Council for Education and Training in Social Work (CCETSW) (1999). *Social Work and Social Change in Northern Ireland*. London: CCETSW.

Clio (2002). *Evaluation of the Core Funding Programme for Victims'/Survivors' Groups*. Belfast: Clio Evaluation Consortium.

Coulter, C. (1999). *Contemporary Northern Irish Society: An Introduction*. London: Pluto.

Crawford, C. (2003). *Inside the UDA: Volunteers and Violence*. London: Pluto.

Cúnamh (2004). www.cunamh.org.

Curran, P., Bell. P., Murray, A. and Loughrey, G. (1990). 'Psychological consequences of the Enniskillin bombing', *British Journal of Psychiatry*, 156, 479–82.

Darby, J. (1995). 'Conflict in Northern Ireland: "A background essay"', in S. Dunn (ed.), *Facets of the Conflict in Northern Ireland*. Basingstoke: Macmillan.

Darby, J. and Williamson, A. (1978). *Violence and the Social Services in Northern Ireland*. London: Heinemann.

Davies, S. (1997). 'The long-term psychological effects of World War Two'. *The Psychologist*, 10(8), 364–7.

Dawes, A., Tredoux, C. and Feinstein, A. (1989). 'Political violence in South Africa: some effects on children of the violent destruction of their community', *International Journal of Mental Health*, 18(2), 16–43.

Department of Health and Social Services (1998). *Living with the Trauma of the 'Troubles'*. Belfast: DHSS.

Department of Health Social Services and Public Safety (2002). *Counselling in Northern Ireland: Report of the Counselling Review*. Belfast: DHSSPS.

deVries, M. (1996). 'Trauma in cultural perspective', in B. van der Kolk, A. McFarlane and L. Weisaeth (eds), *Traumatic Stress: The Effect of Overwhelming Experience on Mind, Body, and Society*. New York: Guilford, 398–413.

Dillenburger, K. (1992). *Violent Bereavement: Widows in Northern Ireland*. Aldershot: Avebury.

Dillenburger, K. (1994). 'Bereavement: a behavioural process', *Irish Journal of Psychology*, 15(4), 524–39.

Dorahy, M. J., Lewis, C. A., Millar, R. G. and Gee, T. L. (2003). 'Predictors of non-pathological dissociation in Northern Ireland: the effects of trauma and exposure to political violence', *Journal of Traumatic Stress*, 16, 611–15.

Farrell, M (1992). *Northern Ireland: The Orange State*. London: Pluto.

Fay, M. T., Morrissey, M. and Smyth, M. (1999). *Northern Ireland's Troubles: The Human Costs*. London: Pluto.

Foster, R. F. (1988). *Modern Ireland 1600–1972*. London: Penguin.

Fredrick, C. (ed.) (1985). *Children Traumatised by Catastrophic Situations*. Washington, D.C.: American Psychiatric Press.

Friedman, M. (1993). 'Psycho-biological and pharmacological approaches to treatment', in J. Wilson and B. Raphael (eds), *International Handbook of Traumatic Stress Syndromes*. New York: Plenum Press, 785–94.

Garbarino, J., Kostelny, K. and DuBrow N. (1991). 'What children can tell us about living in danger', *American Psychologist*, 46(4), 376–83.

Gersons, B. and Carlier, I. (1992). 'Post-traumatic stress disorder: the history of a recent concept', *British Journal of Psychiatry*, 161, 742–8.

Gibson, M. (1996). 'Learning from disasters: the setting up and management of a crisis counselling team', in G. Mulhern and S. Joseph (eds), *Psychosocial Perspectives on Stress and Trauma: From Disaster to Political Violence*. Leicester: British Psychological Society.

Gillespie, K., Duffy, M., Hackmann, A. and Clark, D. M. (2002). 'Community based cognitive therapy in the treatment of post-traumatic stress disorder following the Omagh bomb', *Behaviour Research and Therapy*, 40, 345–57.

Goldberg, D. and Hillier, V. (1979). 'A scaled version of the General Health Questionnaire', *Psychological Medicine*, 9, 139–45.

Goldberg, D. and Williams, P. (1988). *A User's Guide to the General Health Questionnaire*. Windsor: NFER-Nelson.

Gordon, W. A. (1995). *Four Dead in Ohio*. Lake Forest, CA: North Ridge Books.

Green, B. (1993). 'Identifying survivors at risk: trauma and stressors across events', in J. R. Wilson (ed.), *International Handbook of Traumatic Stress Syndromes*. New York: Plenum Press, 135–44.

Hadden, T. (1989). *The Anglo Irish Agreement: Commentary, Text and Official Review*. London: Sweet and Maxwell.

Hadden, W., Rutherford, W. and Merrette, J. (1978). 'The injuries of terrorist bombing: a study of 1,532 consecutive patients', *British Journal of Surgery*, 65, 525–9.

Hamber, B. (1997).'Living with the legacy of impunity: lessons for South Africa about truth, justice and crime in Brazil', *Latin American Report*, 13(2), July–December, 4–16.

—— (ed.) (1998). *Past Imperfect: Dealing with the Past in Northern Ireland and Societies in Transition*. Derry/Londonderry: INCORE.

—— (2000). 'Repairing the irreparable: dealing with the double-binds of making reparations for crimes of the past', *Ethnicity and Health*, 5(3/4), 215–26.

—— (2001). 'Does the truth heal? A psychological perspective on the political strategies for dealing with the legacy of political violence', in N. Biggar (ed.), *Burying the Past: Making Peace and Doing Justice after Civil Conflict*. Washington, D.C.: Georgetown University Press, 131–48.

—— (2003). 'Rights and reasons: Challenges for truth recovery in South Africa and Northern Ireland', *Fordham International Law Journal*, 26(4), 1074–94.

Harvey, J., Orbuch, T., Chwarisz, K. and Garwood, G. (1991). 'Coping with sexual assault: the role of account making and confiding', *Journal of Traumatic Stress*, 4(4), 515–31.

Hayes, P. (1998). 'Post Traumatic Stress Disorder and the "Bloody Sunday" Families'. Paper presented at Magee College, Derry.

—— (2000). *Narrative Tradition, Intergenerational Perceptions of Trauma, Social Identity Development and General Health Implications among a Sample of the 'Bloody Sunday' Families*. Unpublished PhD thesis. Belfast: Queen's University.

Hayes, P. and Campbell, J. (1999), 'Dealing with post traumatic stress disorder: the psychological sequelae of "Bloody Sunday" and the response of state services', *Research on Social Work Practice*, 10, 705–20.

[187]

Herbst, P. (1992). 'From helpless victim to empowered survivor: oral history as a treatment for victims of torture', in *Women and Therapy*. Binghamton, NY: Haworth Press, 141–55.

Herman, J. (1992). *Trauma and Recovery*. New York: Basic Books.

Hillyard, P. (1997). 'Security strategies in Northern Ireland: consolidation or reform?', in C. Gilligan and Jon Tonge (eds), *Peace or War? Understanding the Peace Process in NI*. Aldershot: Ashgate.

Horowitz, M. (1976). *Stress Response Syndromes (1st ed.)*. Northvale, NJ: Jason Aronson.

Horowitz, M. (1993). 'Stress-response syndromes: a review of posttraumatic stress and adjustment disorders', in J. Wilson and B. Raphael (eds), *International Handbook of Traumatic Stress Syndromes*. New York: Plenum Press, 49–60.

Horowitz, M. (1997). *Stress Response Syndromes. (3rd ed.)*. Northvale, NJ: Jason Aronson.

Hough, R. and Vega, W. (1990). 'Mental health consequences of the San Ysidro McDonald's massacre: a community study', *Journal of Traumatic Stress*, 3(1), 71–92.

Hunt, N. (1997). 'Trauma of war', *The Psychologist*, 10(8), 357–60.

Iadicola, P. and Shupa, A. (2003). *Violence, Inequality and Human Freedom*, Chapter 7. Oxford: Rowman and Littlefield.

Janet, P. (1920). *Introduction to the Major Symptoms of Hysteria*. New York: Macmillan.

Joseph, S., Yule, W., Williams, R. and Hodgkinson, P. (1994). 'Correlates of post-traumatic stress at 30 months: the *Herald of Free Enterprise* disaster', *Behaviour Research and Therapy*, 32(5), 521–4.

Kapur, R. (2002). 'Omagh: the beginning of the reparative impulse', *Psychoanalytic Psychotherapy*, 15(3), 265–78.

Kee, M., Bell, P., Loughrey, G., Roddy, R. and Curran, P. (1987). 'Victims of violence: a demographic and clinical study', *Medicine Science and Law*, 27(4), 241–7.

Lindemann, E. (1944). 'Symptomatology and management of acute grief', *American Journal of Psychiatry*, 101, 141–8.

Loughrey, G., Bell, P., Kee, M., Roddy, R. and Curran, P. (1988). 'Posttraumatic stress disorder and civil violence in Northern Ireland', *British Journal of Psychiatry*, 153, 554–60.

Luce, A., Firth-Cozens, J., Midgely, S. and Burges, C. (2002). 'After the Omagh bomb: posttraumatic stress disorder in health service staff', *Journal of Traumatic Stress*, 15(1), 27–30.

Lyons, H. (1971). 'Psychiatric sequelae of the Belfast riots', *British Journal of Psychiatry*, 118(544), 265–73.

Maginnity, R. and Darby, J. (eds) (2002). *Guns and Government: The Management of the Northern Ireland Peace Process*. Basingstoke: Palgrave.

McCafferty, N. (1989). *Peggy Deery: A Derry Family at War*. London: Virago.

McCann, E., Shiels, M. and Hannigan, B. (1992). *Bloody Sunday in Derry: What Really Happened*. Kerry: Brandon.

McClean, R. (1997). *The Road to Bloody Sunday*. Londonderry: Guildhall.

McCoy, K. (1993). 'Integration: a changing scene', Personal Social Services occasional paper 51, Belfast: DHSS.

McFarlane, A. (ed.) (1996). *Resilience, Vulnerability, and the Course of Traumatic Reactions*. New York: Guilford.

McGarry, J. (ed.) (2001). *Northern Ireland and the Divided World: The Northern Ireland Conflict and the Good Friday Agreement in Comparative Perspective*. Oxford: Oxford University Press.

McGarry, J. and O'Leary, B. (1995). *Explaining Northern Ireland: Broken Images*. Oxford: Clarendon.

McGarvey, B. and Collins, S. (2001). 'Can models of post-traumatic stress disorder contribute to the application of cognitive therapy by nurse therapists when dealing with individuals affected by the Omagh bombing? An overview', *Journal of Psychiatric Mental Health Nursing*, 8(6): 477–87.

McGoldrick, M. (1995). *You Can Go Home Again*. New York: Norton.

McKittrick, D. and McVea, D. (2001). *Making Sense of the Troubles*. London: Penguin.

McVeigh, R. (1997). 'Cherishing the children of the nation unequally: sectarianism in Ireland', in P. Clancy, S. Drudy, K. Lynch and L. O'Dowd (eds), *Irish Society: Sociological Perspectives*. Dublin: IPA, 620–51.

McWhirter, L. (1983). 'The Northern Ireland "Troubles": current developmental research perspectives', *Bulletin of the British Psychological Society*, 36, 348–51.

McWhirter, L. and Trew, K. (1982). 'Children in Northern Ireland:

a lost generation?', in J. Anthony and C. Chiland (eds), *The Child in His Family*. New York: Wiley.

Morrissey, M. and Smyth, M. (2002). *Northern Ireland After the Good Friday Agreement: Victims, Grievance and Blame*. London: Pluto.

Mullan, D. (1997). *Eyewitness Bloody Sunday*. Dublin: Wolfhound.

Mullan, K. and Meenan, S. (1997). *I Wasn't Even Born*. Derry: Pat Finucane Centre.

Munck, R. (2000). 'Northern Ireland: from long war to difficult peace?', in R. Munck and P. L. de Silva (eds), *Postmodern Insurgencies*. Basingstoke: Macmillan.

Nagata, D. (1990). 'The Japanese American internment: exploring the trans-generational consequences of traumatic stress', *Journal of Traumatic Stress*, 3(1), 47–69.

Ni Aolain, F. (2000). *The Politics of Force: Conflict Management and State Violence in Northern Ireland*. Belfast: Blackstaff.

Northern Ireland Office (1998a). *The Agreement (Command Paper 3883)*. Belfast: NIO.

—— (1998b). *We Will Remember Them: Report of the Northern Ireland Victims Commissioner, Sir Kenneth Bloomfield*. Belfast: Northern Ireland Office.

—— (2001). *Victim Policy for a New Era: Developing a Comprehensive Victims Strategy* (consultation paper). Belfast: Northern Ireland Office.

—— (2003). www.nio.gov.uk/digestinfo.pdf

Ochberg, F. (1993). 'Posttraumatic therapy', in J. Wilson and B. Raphael (eds), *International Handbook of Traumatic Stress Syndromes*. New York: Plenum Press, 773–84.

O'Dowd, L., Rolston, B. and Tomlinson, M. (1980). *Northern Ireland: Between Civil Rights and Civil War*. London: CSE Books.

Office of the First and Deputy First Minister for Northern Ireland (2002a). *Consultation Paper on a Victims' Strategy*. Belfast: OFDFM.

—— (2002b). *Reshape, Rebuild, Achieve*. Belfast: OFDFM.

—— (2002c). *The Report of the Healing Through Remembering Project*. Belfast: OFDFM.

—— (2003). www.victimsni.gov.uk/responses.pdf

Orner, R. (1997). 'Falklands war veterans', *The Psychologist*, 10(8), 351–5.

Patton, M. (1990). *Qualitative Evaluation and Research Methods.* Beverly Hills, CA: Sage.

Pinkerton, J. and Campbell, J. (2002). 'Social work and social justice in Northern Ireland: towards a new occupational space', *British Journal of Social Work*, 32, 723–37.

Pringle, P. and Jacobson, P. (2000). *Those Are Real Bullets, Aren't They?: Bloody Sunday, Derry, 30 January, 1972.* London: Fourth Estate.

Probert, B. (1978). *Beyond Orange and Green: The Political Economy of the Northern Ireland Crisis.* London: Zed.

Purdy, B. (1990). *Politics in the Streets: The Origins of the Civil Rights Movement in Northern Ireland.* Belfast: Blackstaff.

Pynoos, R. (1985). 'Interaction of trauma and grief in childhood', in S. Eth and R. Pynoos (eds), *Posttraumatic Stress Disorder in Children.* Washington, D.C.: American Psychiatric Press, 171–86.

Pynoos, R. and Nader, K. (1993). 'Issues in the treatment of post-traumatic stress in children and adolescents', in J. Wilson and B. Raphael (eds), *International Handbook of Traumatic Stress Syndromes.* New York: Plenum Press, 535–50.

Reilly, I. (2000). 'Legacy: people and poets from Northern Ireland', *Australian and New Zealand Journal of Family Therapy*, 21(3).

Riessman, C. (1993). *Narrative Analysis.* Newbury Park, CA: Sage.

Rolston, B. (2000). *Unfinished Business: State Killings and the Quest for Truth.* Belfast: Beyond the Pale.

Roth, S. and Lebowitz, L. (1988). 'The experience of sexual trauma', *Journal of Traumatic Stress*, 1(1), 79–107.

Scott, R., Brooks, N. and McKinley, W. (1995). 'Post-traumatic morbidity in a civilian community of litigants: a follow-up at 3 years', *Journal of Traumatic Stress*, 8(3), 403–17.

Scratton, P. (ed.) (2002). *Beyond September 11: An Anthology of Dissent.* London: Pluto.

Shepherd, J. (1992). 'Posttraumatic stress disorder in Vietnamese women', *Women and Therapy*, 13(3), 281–96.

Shevlin, M. and McGuigan, K. (2003). 'The long-term psychological impact of Bloody Sunday on families of the victims as measured by the Revised Impact of Event scale', *British Journal of Clinical Psychology*, 42(4), 427–32.

Smyth, M. and Campbell, J. (1996). 'Social work, sectarianism and anti-sectarian practice in Northern Ireland', *British Journal of Social Work*, 26(1), 77–92.

Smyth, M. and Hayes, P. (1994). 'Posttraumatic stress and the case of the "Bloody Sunday" families'. Paper presented at the *Conflict in Mental Health* Conference, The Queen's University of Belfast.

Smyth, M., Morrissey, M. and Hamilton, J. (2001). *Caring Through the Troubles: Health and Social Services in North and West Belfast*. Belfast: North and West Belfast Health and Social Services Trust.

Smyth, M. and Robinson, G. (eds) (2001). *Researching Violently Divided Societies: Ethical and Methodological Issues*. London: Pluto.

Solkoff, N. (1981). 'Children of the survivors of the Nazi holocaust: a critical review of the literature', *American Journal of Orthopsychiatry*, 51, 29–42.

—— (1992). 'Children of survivors of the Nazi holocaust: A critical review of the literature', *American Journal of Orthopsychiatry*, 62(3), 342–58.

Stallard, P. and Law, F. (1994). 'The psychological effects of trauma on children', *Children and Society*, 8(2), 89–97.

Stewart, A. T. Q. (1977). *The Narrow Ground: Aspects of Ulster, 1609–1969*. London: Faber.

Stone, M. (1985). 'Shellshock and the psychologist', in W. Bynum, R. Porter and M. Shepard (eds), *The Anatomy of Madness: Essays in the History of Psychiatry. Vol. II, Institutions and Society*. London: Tavistock.

Sukla, J. A. (ed.) (2000). *Death Squad: The Anthropology of State Terror*. Philadelphia: UPP.

Sutton, M. (1994). *An Index of Deaths from the Conflict in Ireland 1969–1993*. Belfast: Beyond the Pale.

Swartz, L. (1998). *Culture and Mental Health: A South African View*. Oxford: Oxford University Press.

Taylor, P. (1997). *The Provos: the IRA and Sinn Fein*. London: Bloomsbury.

Teague, P. (ed.) (1993). *The Economy of Northern Ireland: Perspectives for Structural Change*. London: Lawrence and Wishart.

Terr, L. (1990). *Too Scared to Cry: How Trauma Affects Children and Ultimately Us All*. New York: Basic Books.

Tilley, C. (2002). 'Violent and nonviolent trajectories in contentious politics', in K. Worcester, S. A. Bemanzohn and M. Ungar (eds), *Violence and Politics*. London: Routledge.

Toner, I. (1990). 'Personality profiles of Belfast children', paper presented at the *European Conference on Developmental Psychology*, Stirling, Scotland.

—— (1994). 'Children of the "Troubles" in Northern Ireland: perspectives and intervention', *International Journal of Behavioural Development*, 17(4), 629–47.

Traynor, C. (1998). 'Social work in a sectarian society', in M. Anderson, S. Bogues, J. Campbell, H. Douglas and M. McColgan (eds), *Social Work and Social Change in Northern Ireland*. London: CCETSW.

Truth and Reconciliation Commission of South Africa (1998). *Report*, Vol 3, Chapter 6.

van der Kolk, B. (1994). 'The body keeps the score: memory and the evolving psychobiology of posttraumatic stress', *Harvard Review of Psychiatry*, 1(5), 253–65.

van der Kolk, B. and Fisler, R. (1995). 'Dissociation and the fragmentary nature of traumatic memories: overview and exploratory study', *Journal of Traumatic Stress*, 8, 505–25.

van der Kolk, B. and van der Hart, O. (1991). 'The intrusive past: the flexibility of memory and the engraving of trauma', *American Image*, 48(4), 425–54.

Walsh, D. P. J. (2000). *Bloody Sunday and the Rule of Law in Northern Ireland*. Dublin: Gill and Macmillan.

Walsh, D. (2002). 'Bloody Sunday Inquiry progressed praised' http://news.bbc.co.uk/1/hi/in_depth/northern_ireland/2000/bloody_sunday_inquiry/1789319.stm on 30/1/2002.

Waugh, M. (1997). 'Keeping the home fires burning', *The Psychologist*, 10(8), 361–3.

Weine, S., Becker, D., McGlashan, T., Vojvoda, D., Hartman, S. and Robbins, J. (1995). 'Adolescent survivors of "ethnic cleansing": observations on the first year in America', *American Academy of Child and Adolescent Psychiatry*, 34(9), 1153–9.

Weiss, D. and Marmar, C. (1997). 'The impact of Event Scale – revised', *Psychosomatic Medicine*, 41, 209–18.

Whyte, J. (1983). 'Control and supervision of urban 12-year-olds within and outside Northern Ireland: a pilot study', *Irish*

Journal of Psychology, 6(1), 37–45.

Whyte, J. (1991). *Interpreting Northern Ireland.* Oxford: Clarendon.

Widgery (1972). *Report of the Tribunal appointed to inquire into the events on Bloody Sunday, 30 January 1972, which led to loss of life in connection with the procession in Londonderry on that day by the Rt. Hon. Lord Widgery, OBE, TD.* London: HMSO.

Wilson, R. and Cairns, E. (1987). 'Political violence, perception of violence, and psychological disorder in Northern Ireland', paper presented at the British Association for the Advancement of Science, Belfast.

Yule, W. (1989). 'The effects of disasters on children', *Association for Child Psychology and Psychiatry Newsletter,* 11(6), 3–6.

Yule, W. (1994a). 'Posttraumatic stress disorders', in M. Rutter, E. Taylor and L. Hersov (eds), *Child and Adolescent Psychiatry – Modern Approaches.* Oxford: Blackwell.

Yule, W. (1994b). 'Posttraumatic stress disorder', in T. H. Ollendick, N. J. King and W. Yule (eds), *International Handbook of Phobic and Anxiety Disorders in Children and Adolescents.* New York: Plenum Press.

Index

9/11 4, 29

A
accountability, democratic 35
addiction to drugs 54
alcohol, use of 41, 76, 86, 123–4,
  137, 142, 177
American Psychiatric Association
  38, 40, 58, 60, 74, 82, 89, 90,
  99
Amnesty International 26, 27, 33
anger, post-traumatic 53–4,
  79–80, 100–2, 134
Anglican church 10
Anglo-Irish Agreement (1985) 21
Anglo-Irish War (1919–21) 10
anniversary marches 1
antidepressant drugs 45, 54–5,
  123
  see also medication
anti-violent ethos 6, 51, 94,
  103–7, 178–9
anxiety 50, 52
apoliticism 103–7, 178–9
Apprentice Boys 11
  Marches 14
Army, British 15, 33, 146, 149,
  158, 168
  deaths caused by 32, 33 (see
  also deaths)
  numbers in Northern Ireland
  20
  use in Northern Ireland 13,
  14, 16–21
  see also Parachute Regiment
Aron, A. 3, 56
arrest, powers of 34
art therapy 49, 53

Arthur, P. 13
Ayalon, O. 109

B
B Specials 14, 81
Ballykelly 21
Ballymoney 22
Banks, M. 61, 62
Bardon, J. 16
baton charges/rounds 14, 33
Belfast 14–15, 17, 20, 22, 110
  bank robbery (2004) 23
  see also Falls Road
Belfast Agreement (1998) 5,
  22–4, 32, 35–6, 114, 116, 169
Bell, P. 39
Bew, P. 10, 12, 13
Birmingham 21
  Birmingham Six 103
Birrell, C. 111
Blair, Tony 7, 135, 145, 147
blame 54, 117
  for Bloody Sunday 145,
  146–7, 167–72, 180
  of Bloody Sunday victims
  174, 176
  of self 40, 50, 51
Blease, M. 52, 95
Bloody Friday 20
Bloody Sunday
  25th anniversary 62, 63, 73,
  129, 144, 177
  30th anniversary 64, 66,
  129–43, 179
  bias in attitudes 3, 9
  catalyst for later Troubles 3
  comparable events 27–8
  context 9–24

[195]

McGarry, J. 11, 12, 113
McGarvey, B. 39
McGoldrick, M. 3
McGuigan, Bernard xvii, 18
McGuigan, K. 39, 47, 66
McKinley, W. 44, 45
McKinney, Gerard xvii, 19
McKinney, William xvii, 19
McKittrick, D. 12, 15, 16, 19, 20, 32
McLaughlin, J. 111
McVea, D. 12, 15, 16, 19, 20, 32
McVeigh, R. 10, 12
McWhirter, L. 58
media coverage 1, 51, 70, 76, 87, 92, 129, 176
    of the Saville Inquiry 140–3, 149
medication, use of 45, 54–5, 76
    see also antidepressant drugs, Valium
Meenan, Sharon xvii
memorial to victims 115, 118
memory
    'active' 91
    lapses 88, 76, 86, 88
    lost/repressed 74
Merrette, J. 3, 21
Miami Showband killings 21
Monaghan 21
Morrissey, M. 13, 19, 32, 112, 113, 114, 117, 153
mourning 41, 47–9
Mullan, D. 1, 17, 18, 70, 144, 145
Mullan, Killian xvii
Munck, R. 27
Murie, A. 111
Myers, C. S. 39

N
Nader, K. 49, 50, 52, 53, 77

Nagata, D. 3, 58
nail bombs 16, 82, 161
narrative, role of 5, 32, 55–6, 59, 117
    see also life story
Nash, William xvii, 19
Nationalism 10, 15
Nelson, Rosemary 34
Newry 21
Ni Aolain, F. 31, 33, 34, 36
non-conformism 10
Northern Ireland
    creation and definition 10, 26, 31
    devolved administration 12, 20
    Direct Rule 20, 111, 112
    economics/problems 11, 23
    geopolitics 12
    government spending 11, 110, 116–17
    health and social services 109–28
    history of conflict 11–20
    power sharing 20–1, 22, 36
    quangos and NGOs 111, 125–8
    state violence 30–5
Northern Ireland Assembly 113
Northern Ireland Civil Rights Association (NICRA) 14, 16, 146
Northern Ireland Human Rights Commission 36
Northern Ireland Labour Party 11
Northern Ireland Office 115–16
NUD*IST 66–7
numbness following trauma 40, 83–5

O
Ochberg, F. 54